THIS JOU BELONGS TO:

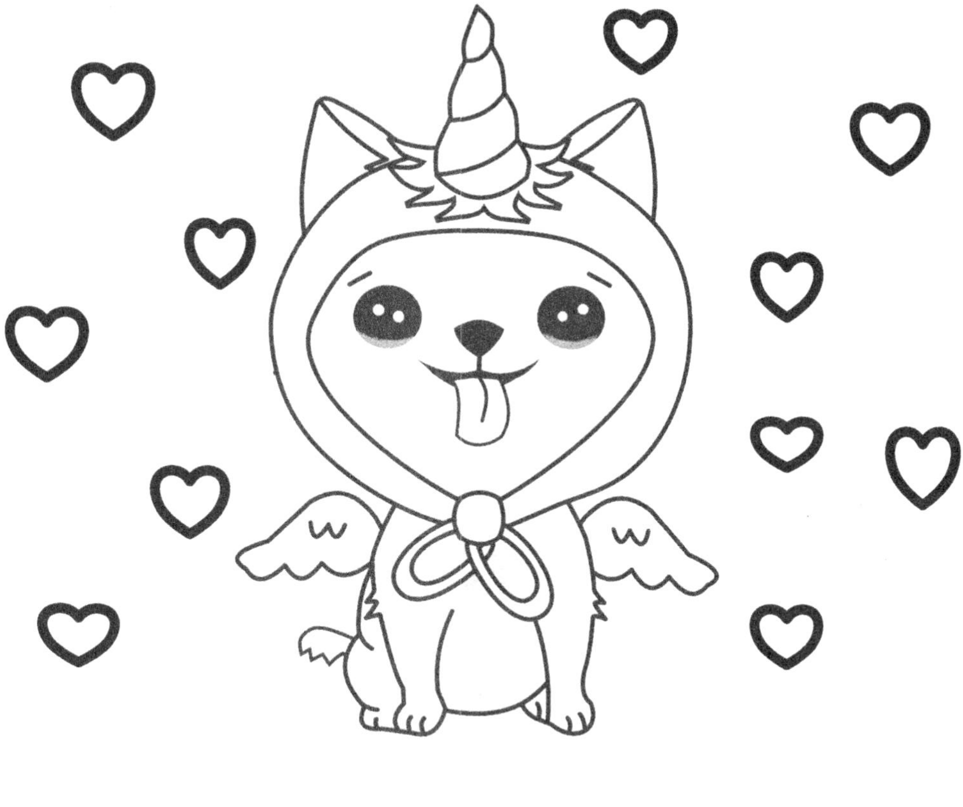

CORGI + UNICORN = CORGICORN

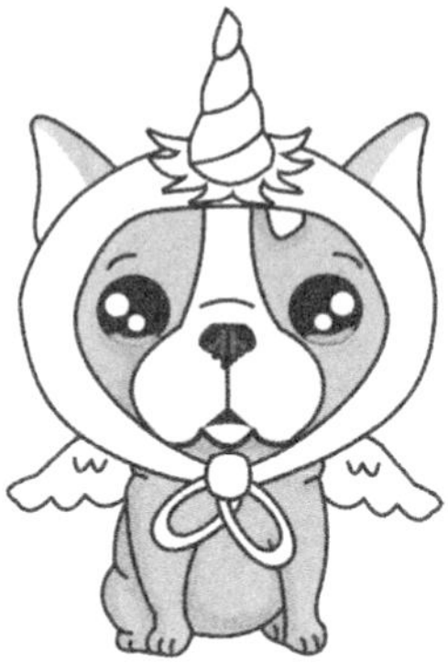

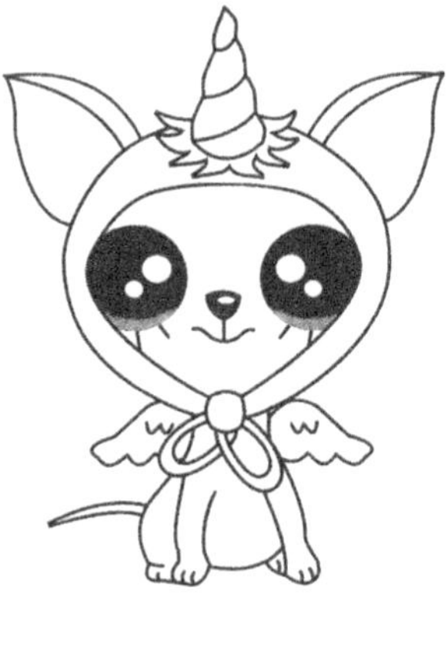

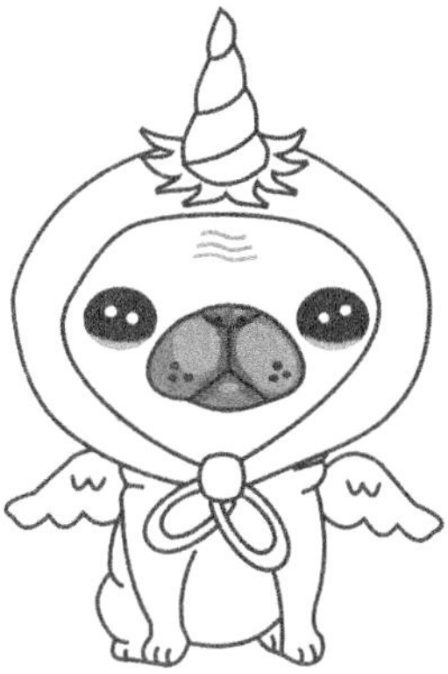

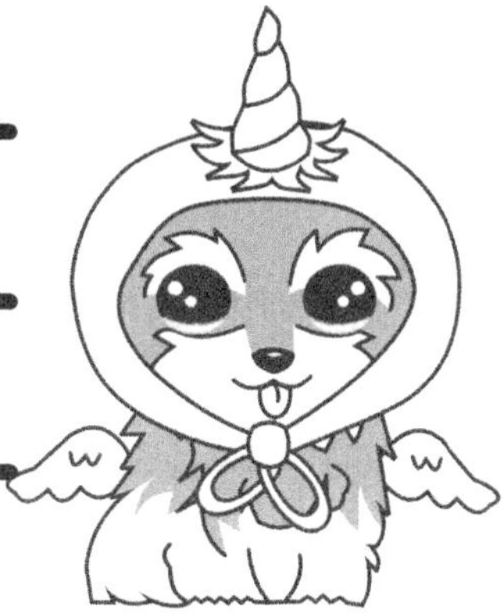

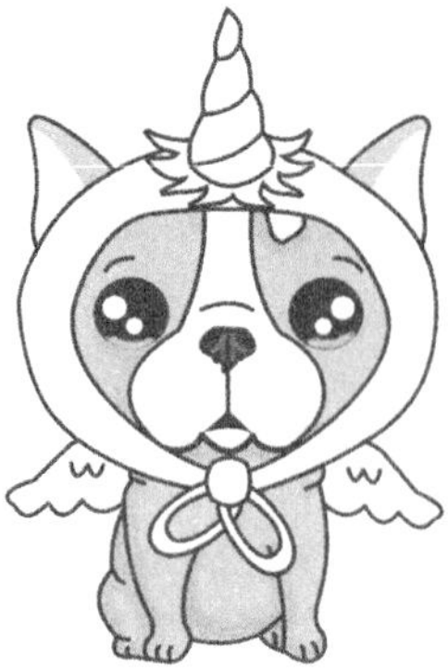

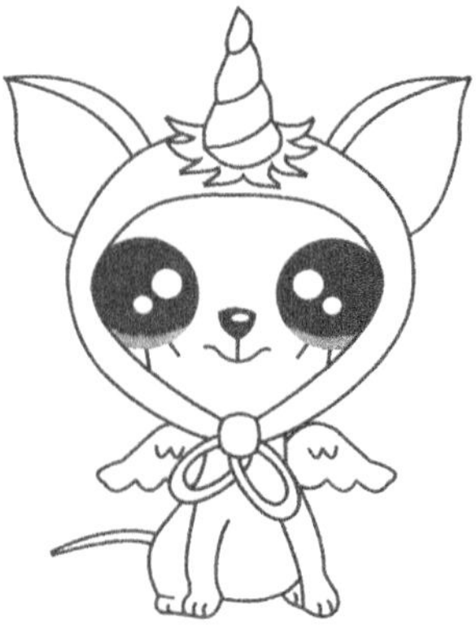

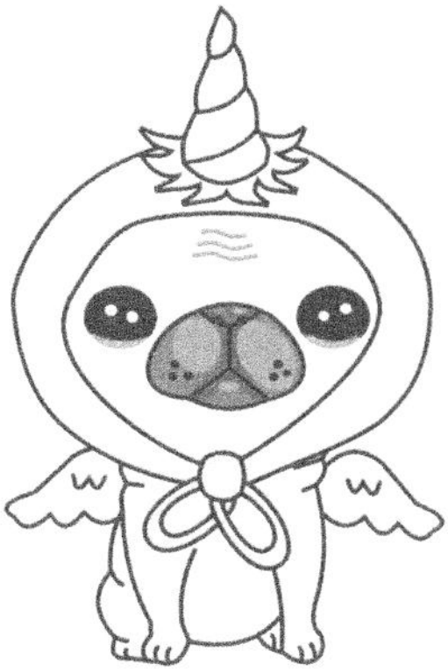

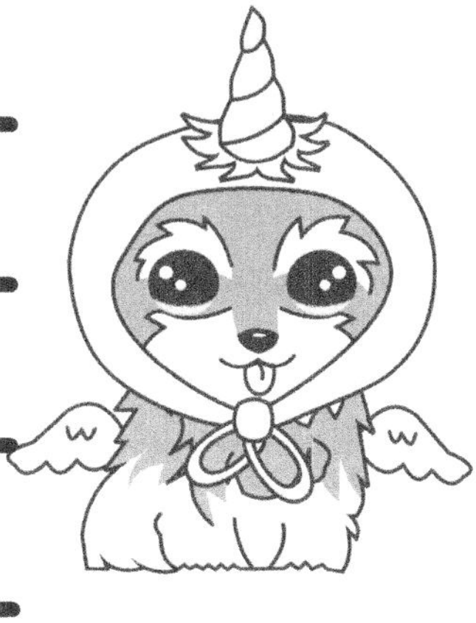

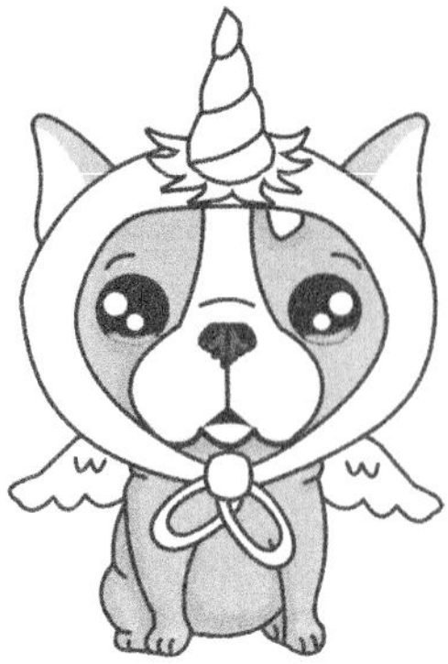

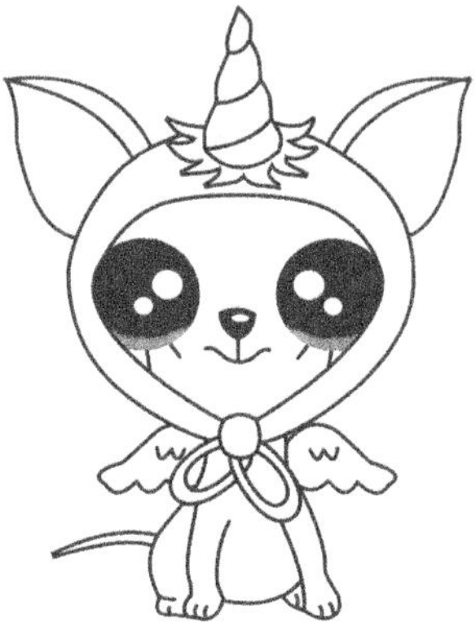

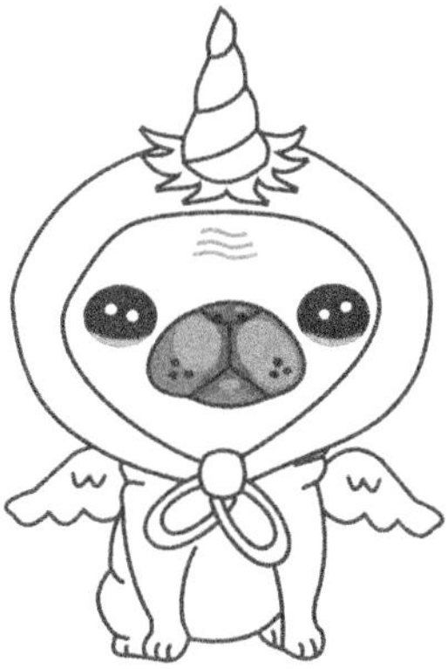

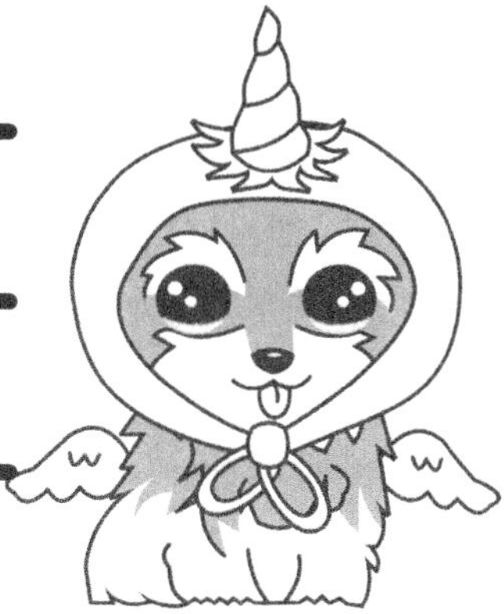

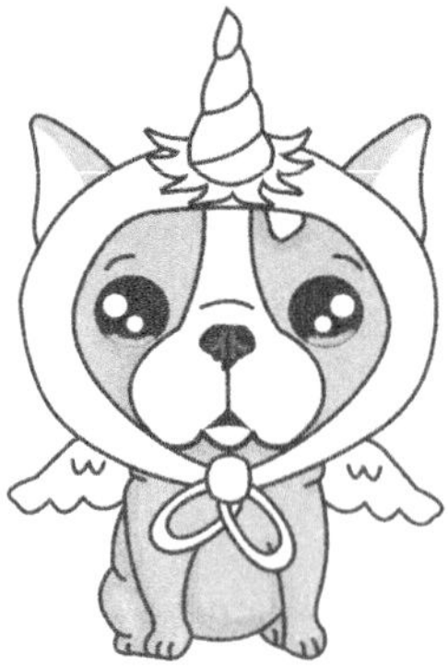

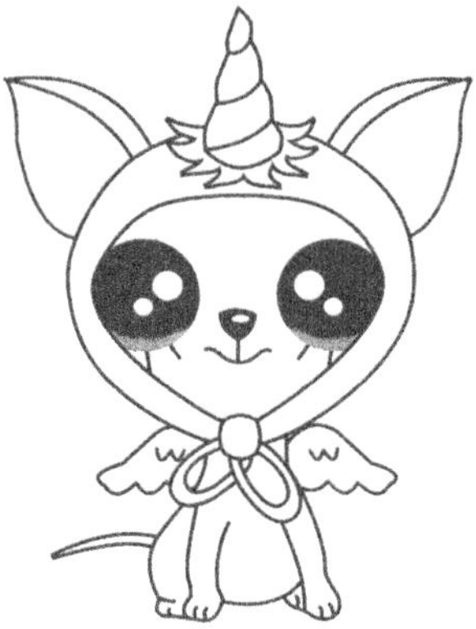

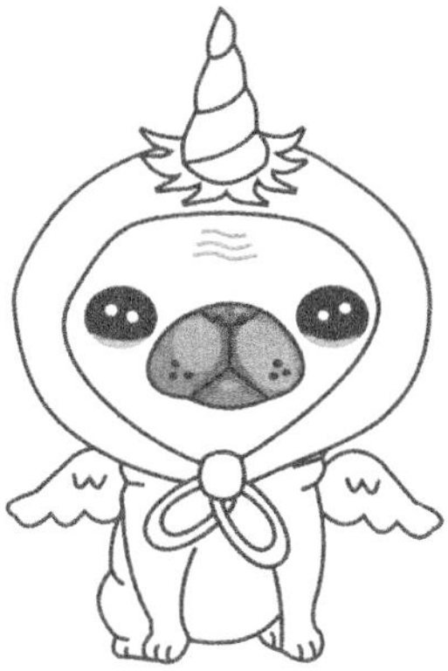

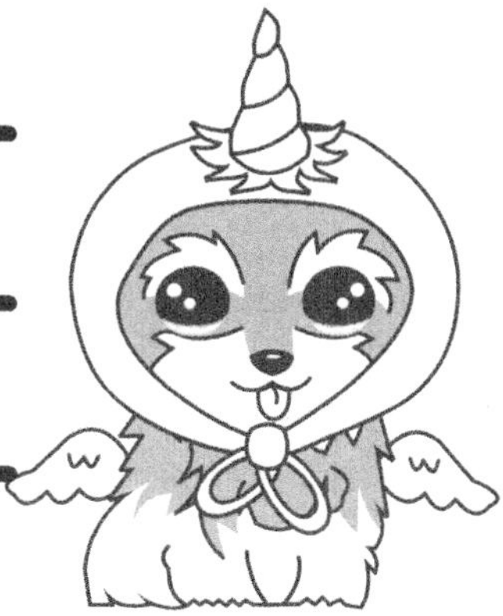

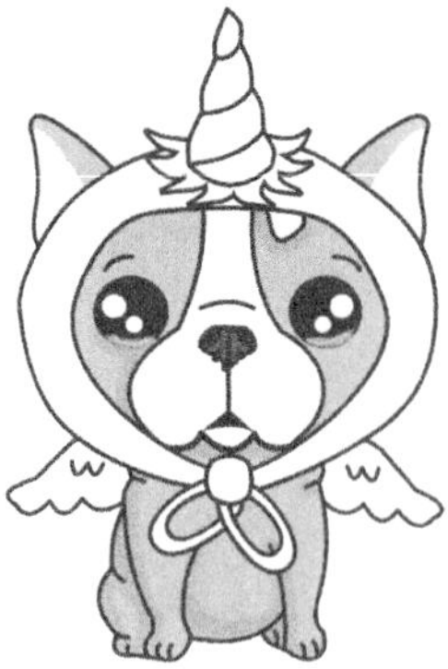

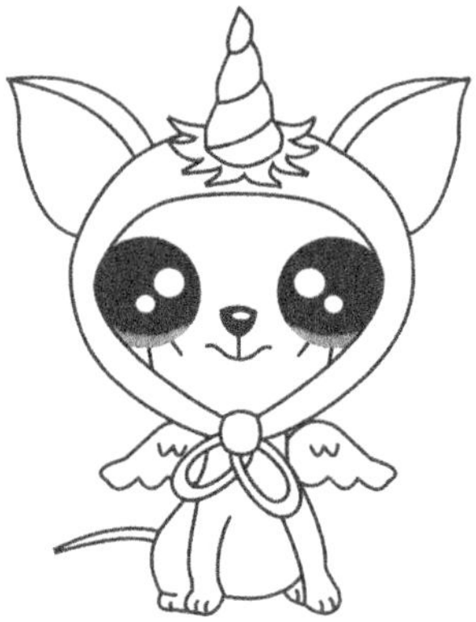

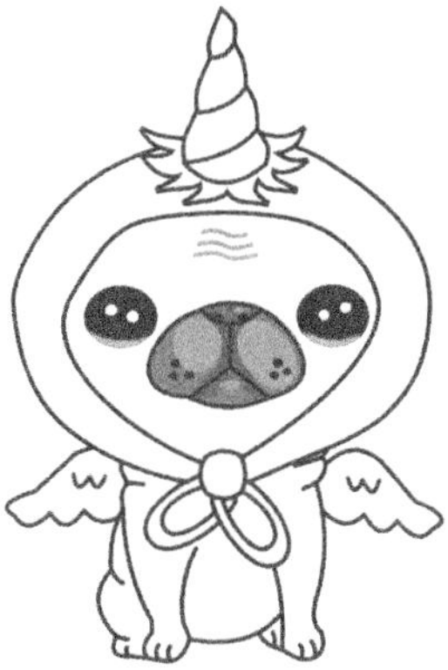

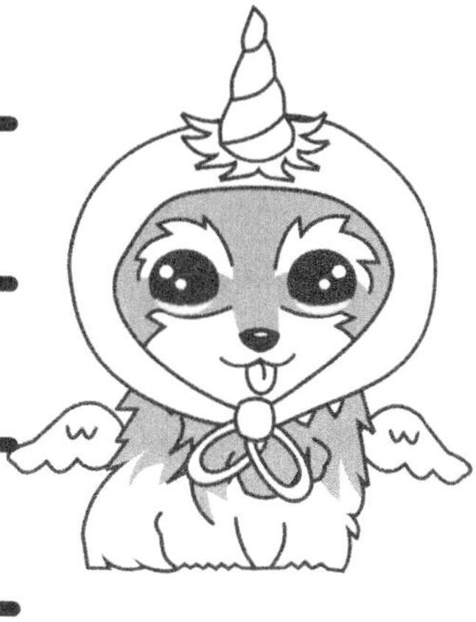

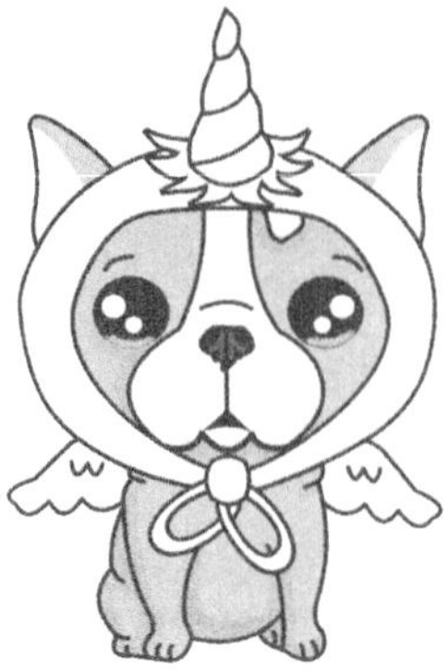

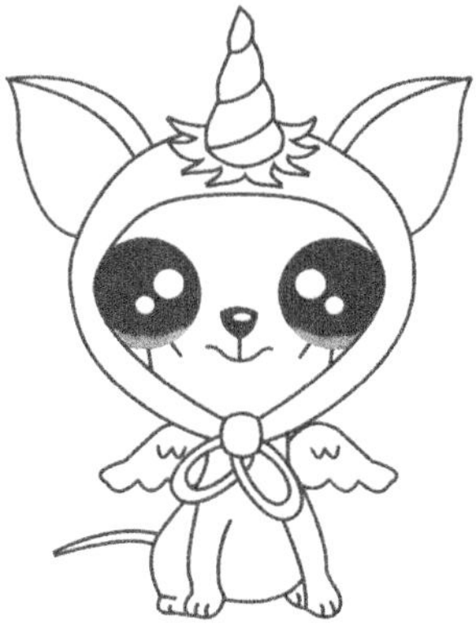

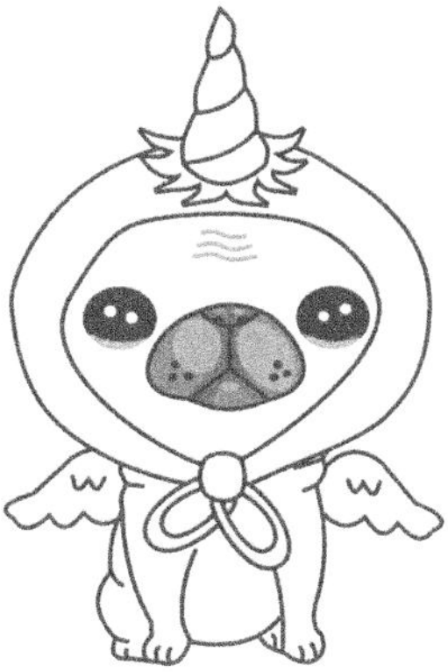

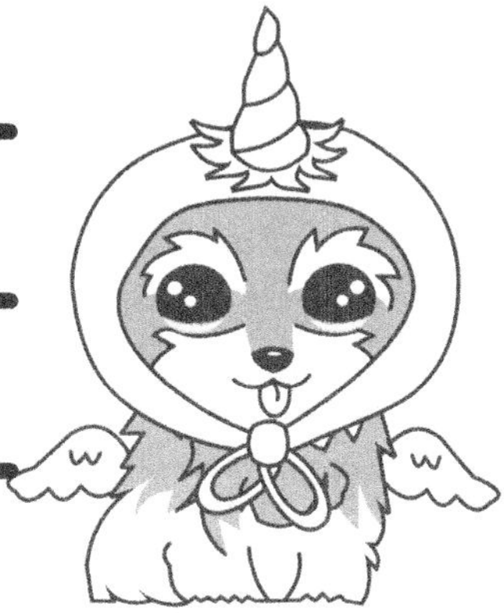

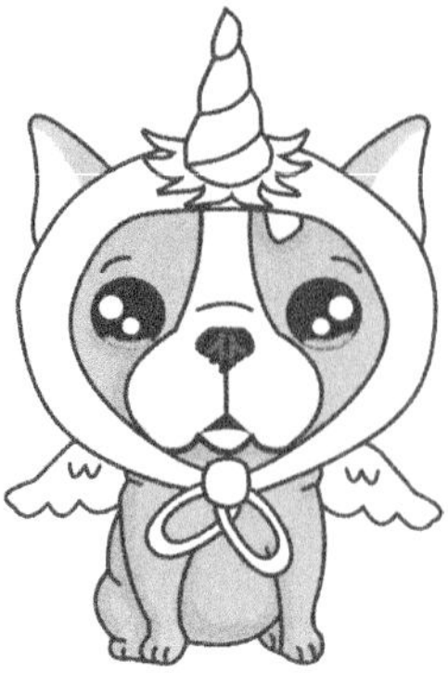

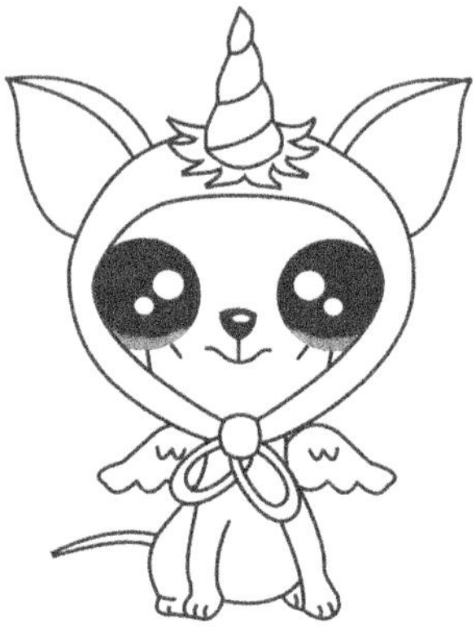

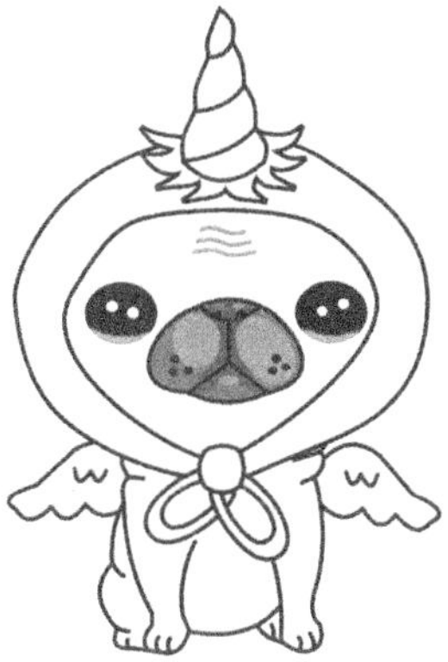

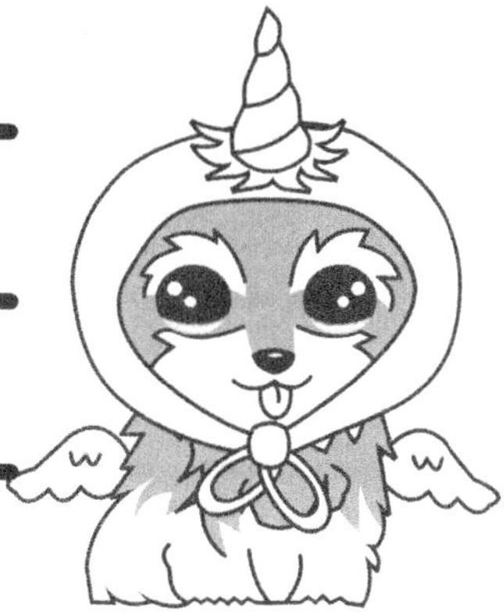

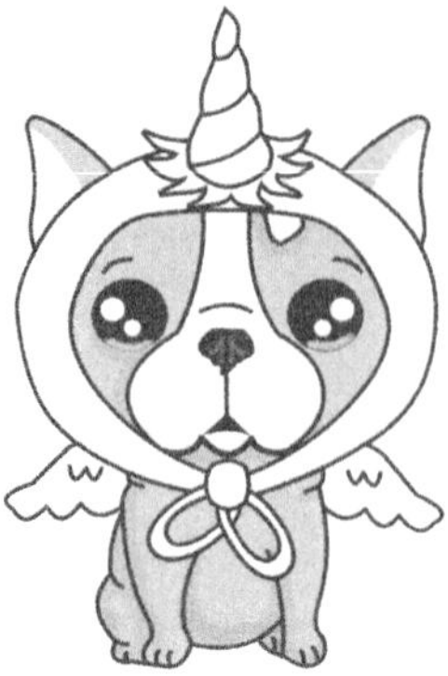

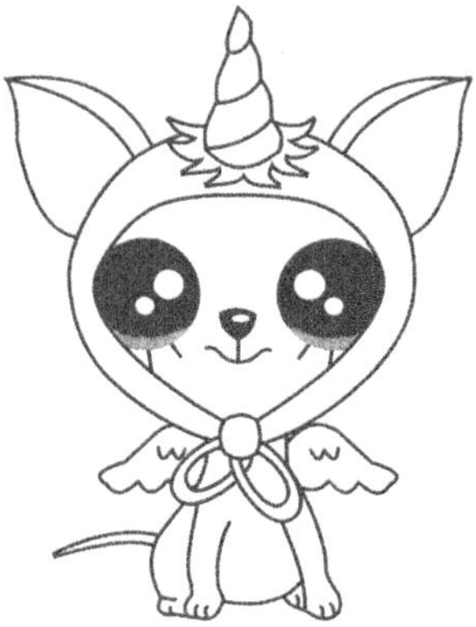

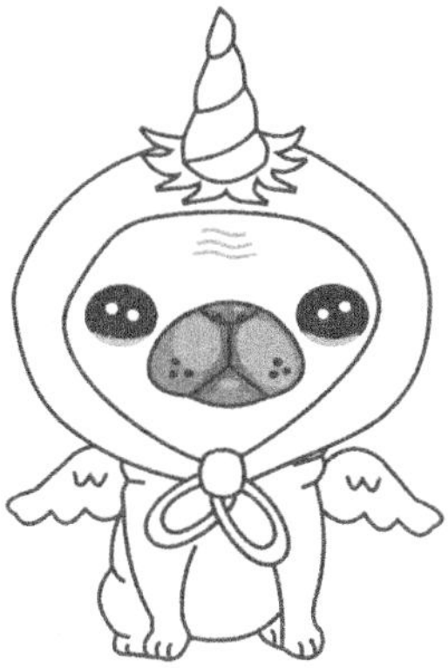

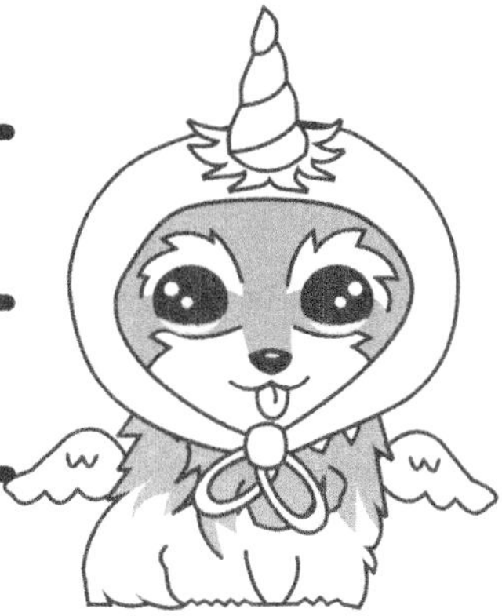

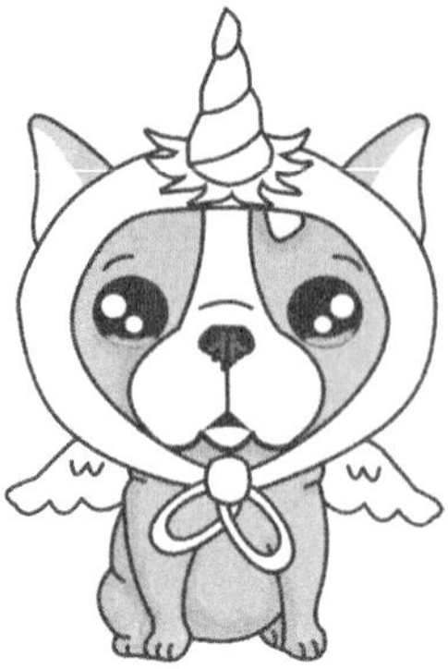

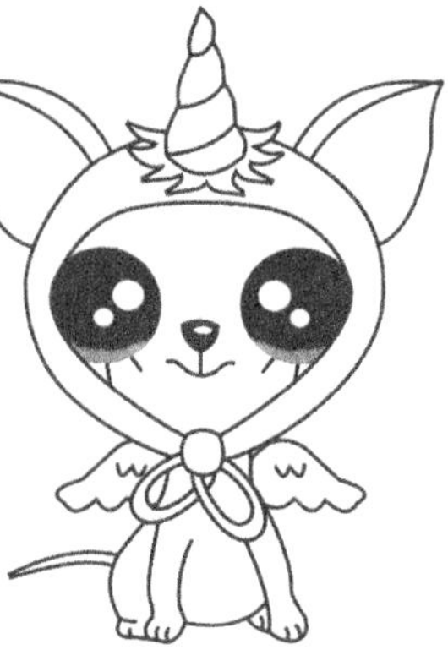

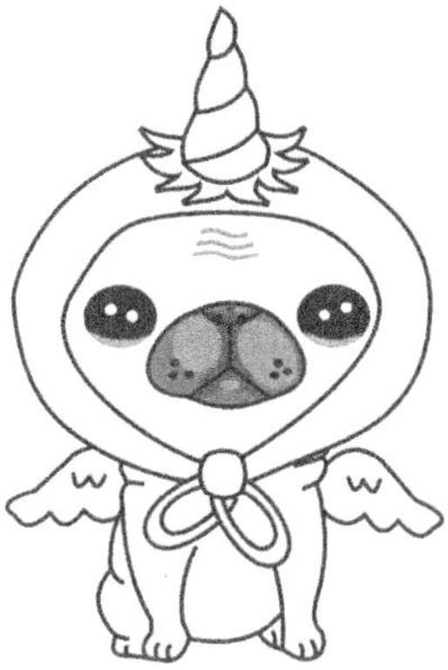

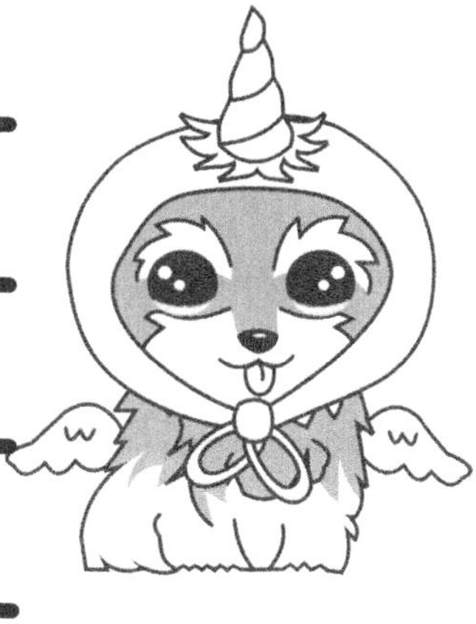

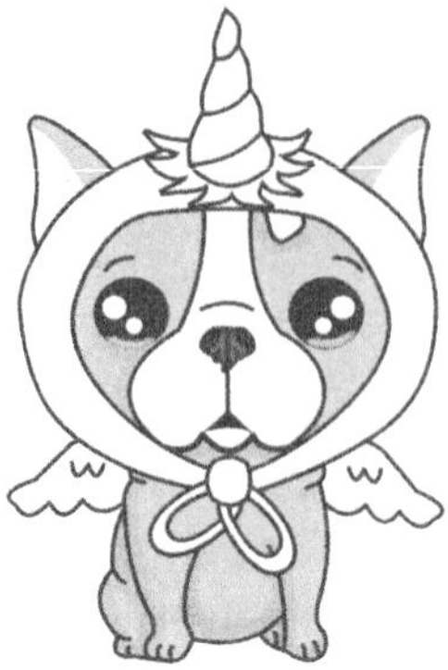

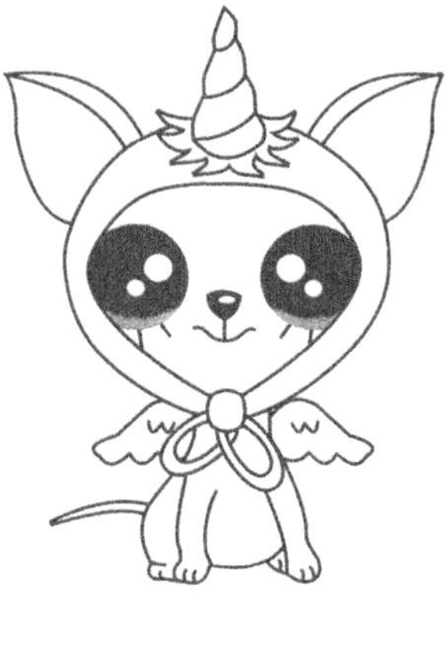

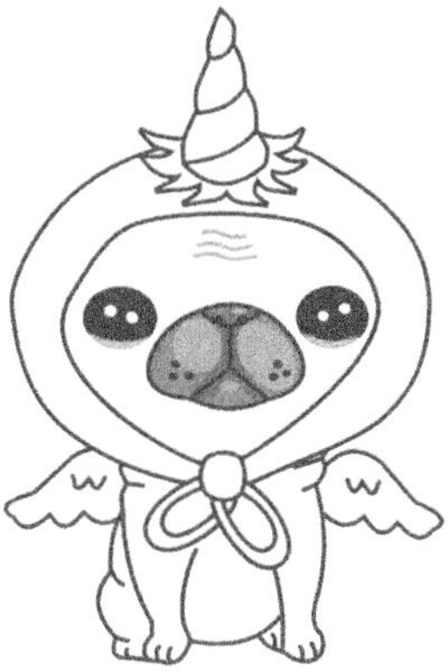

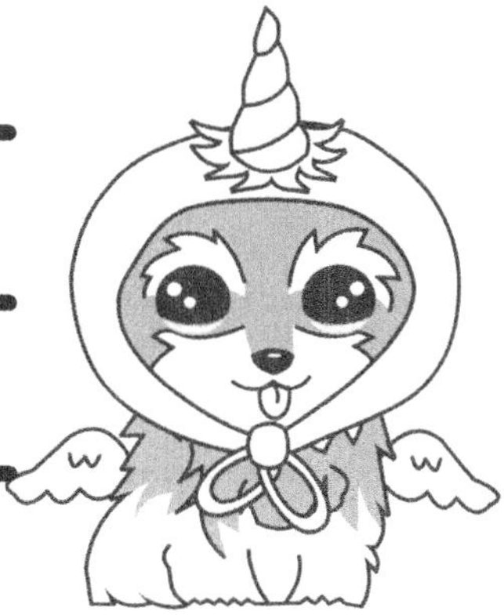

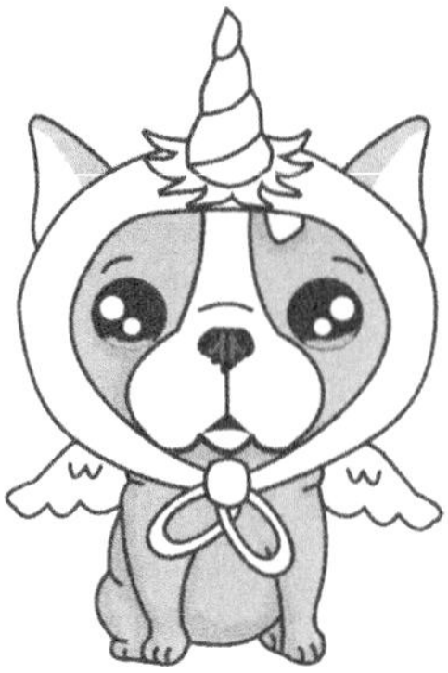

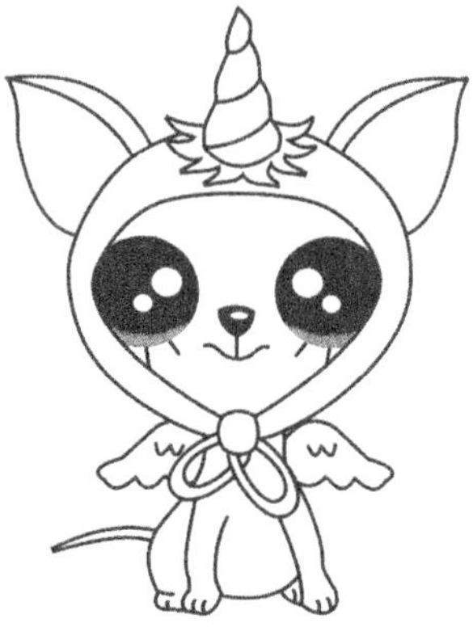

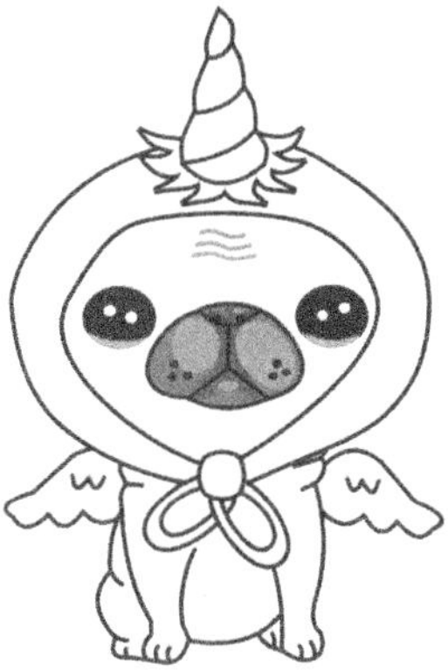

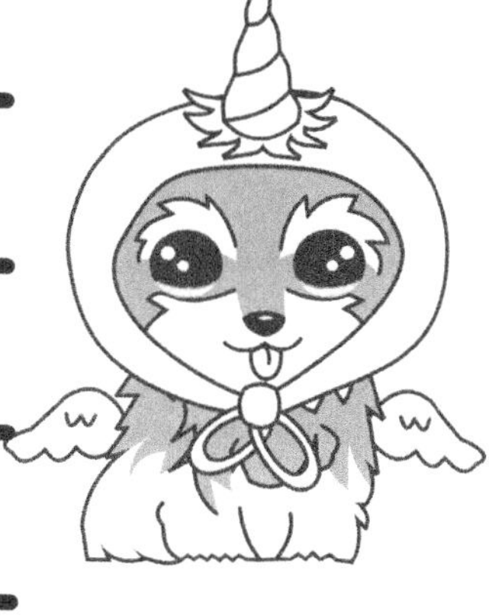

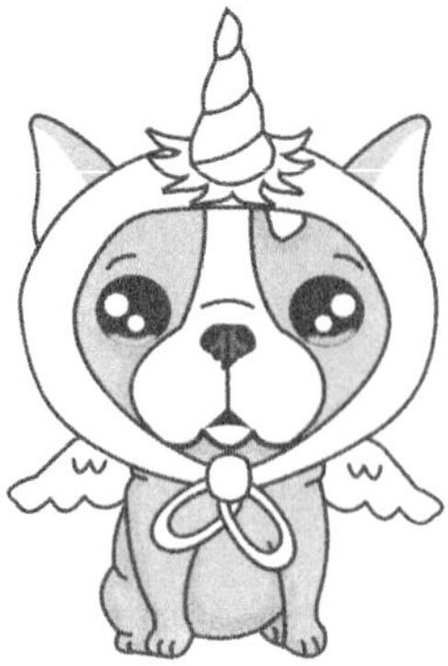

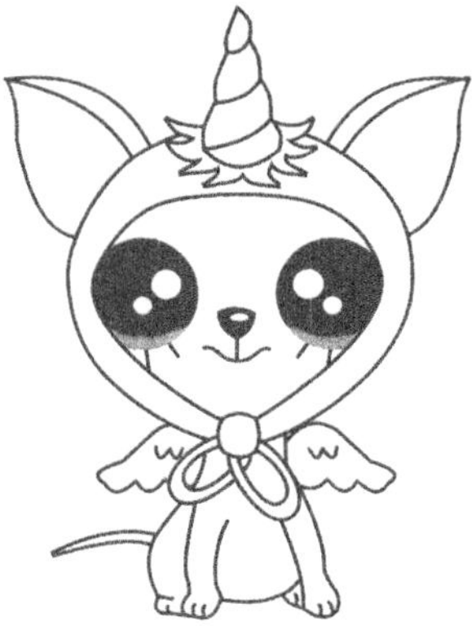

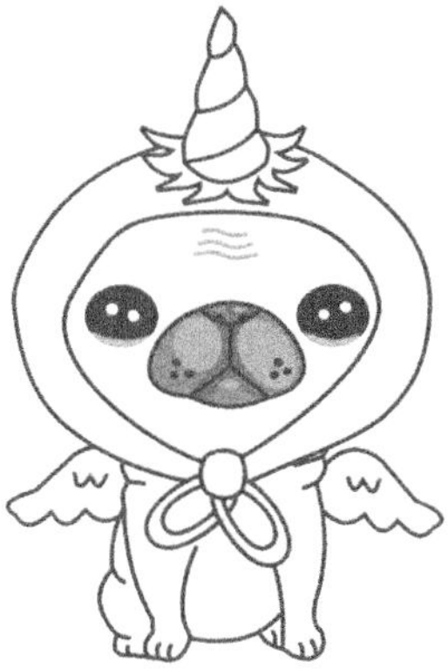

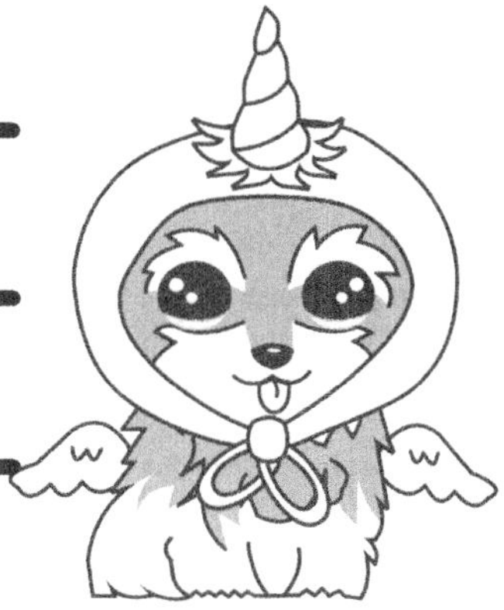

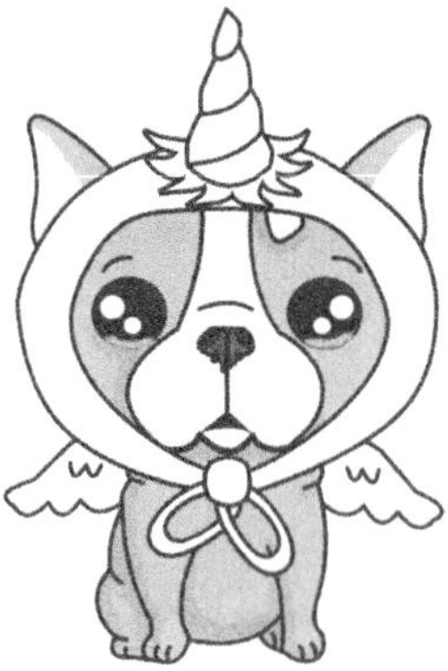

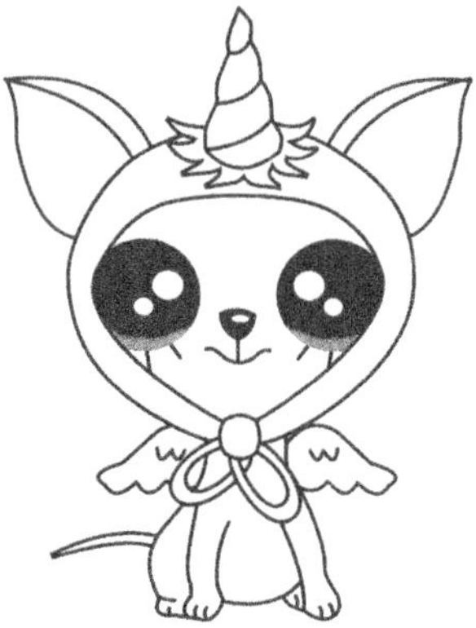

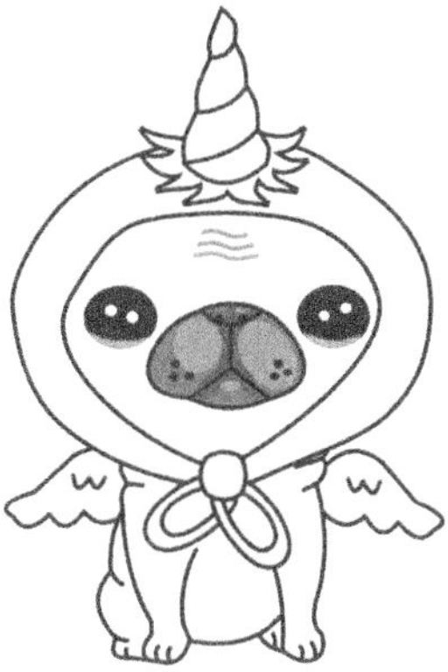

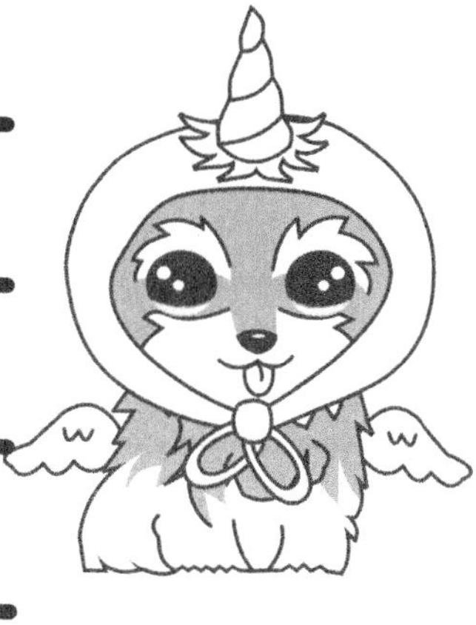

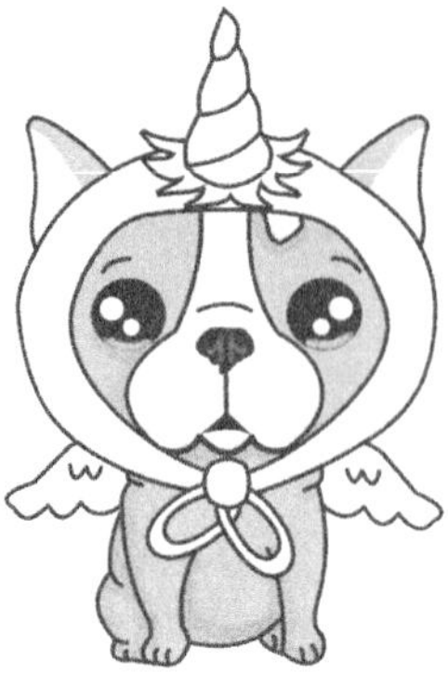

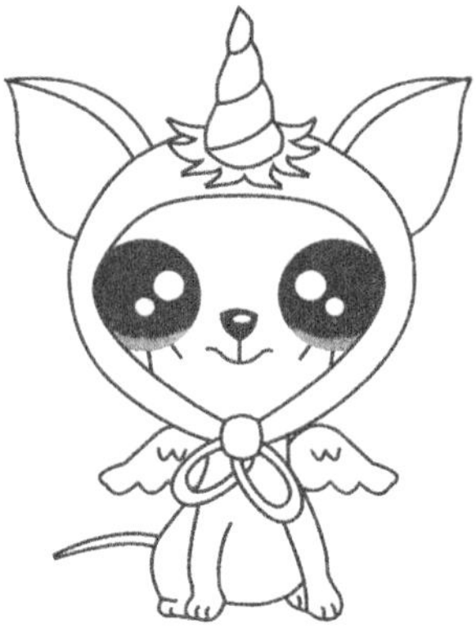

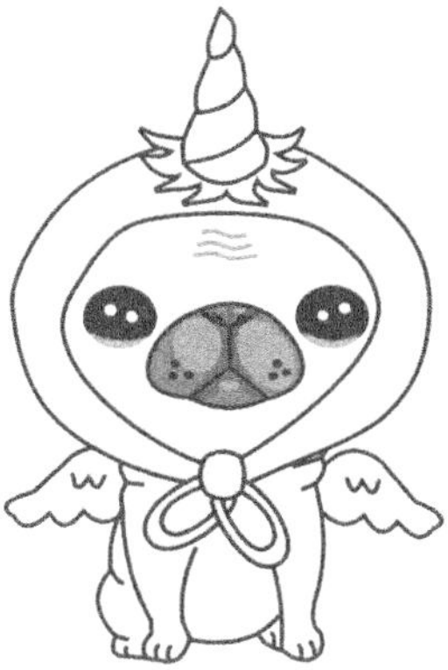

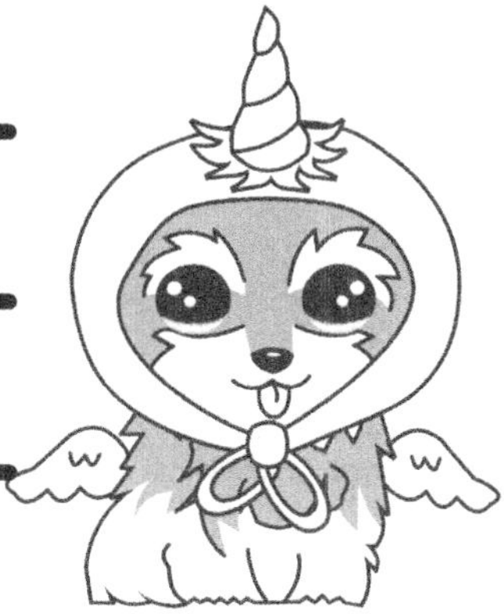

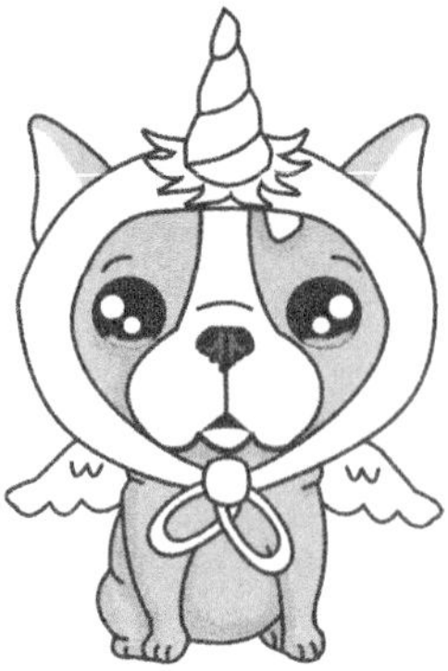

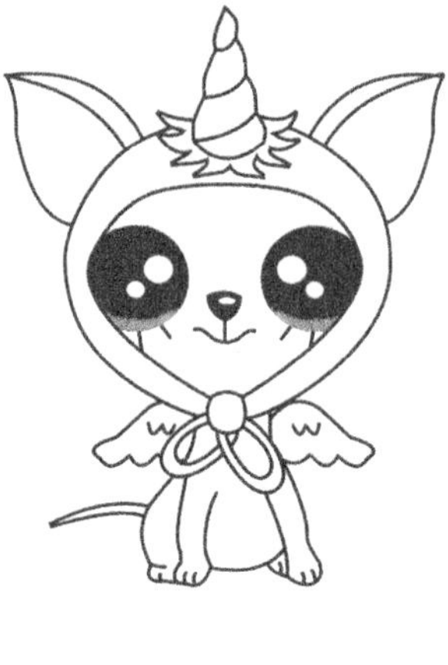

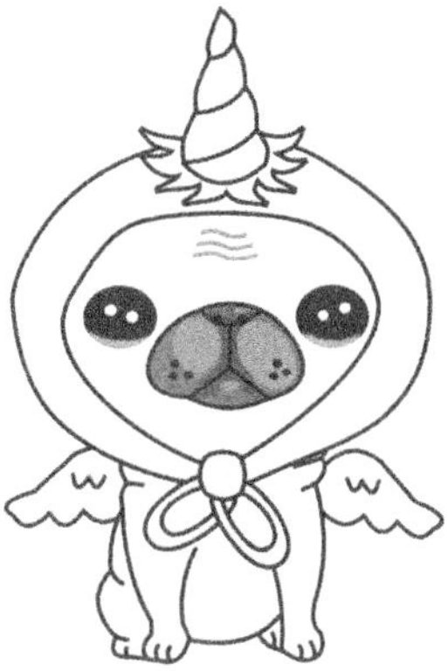

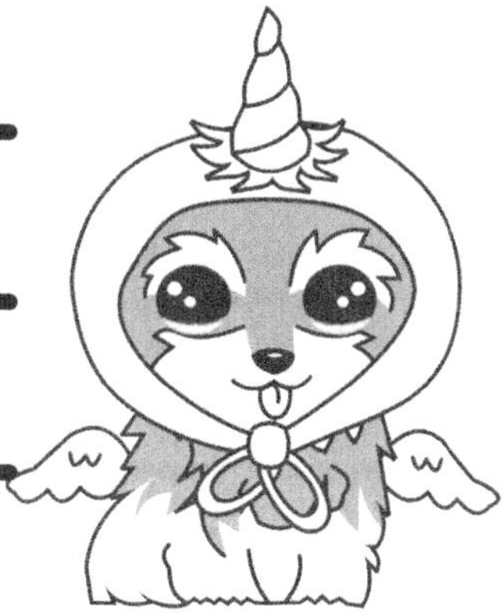

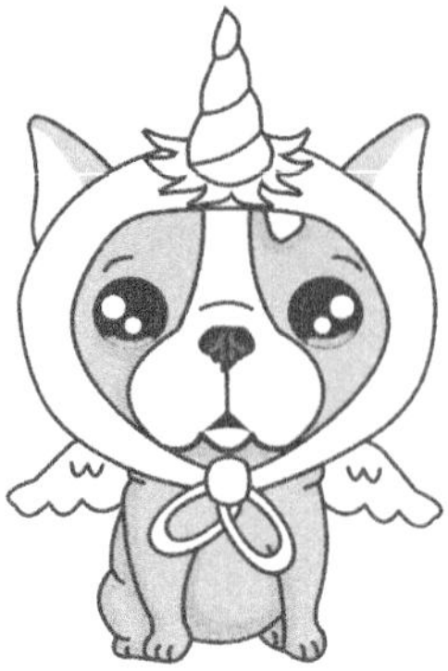

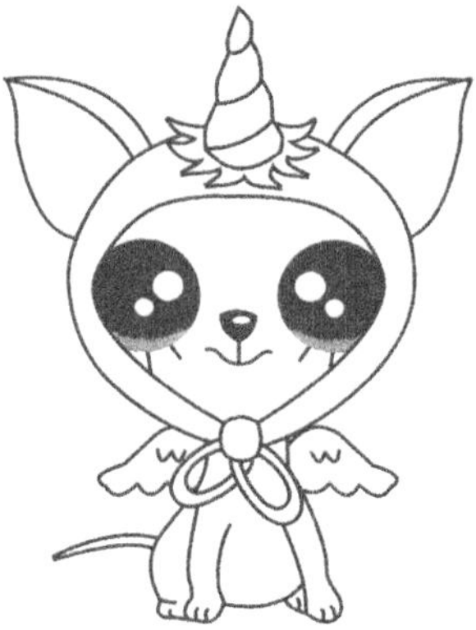

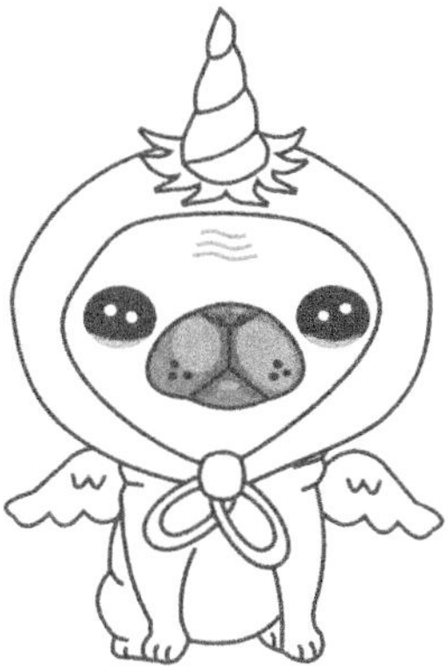

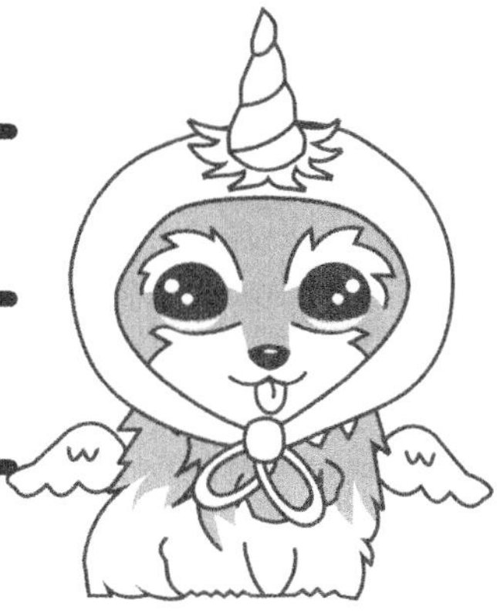

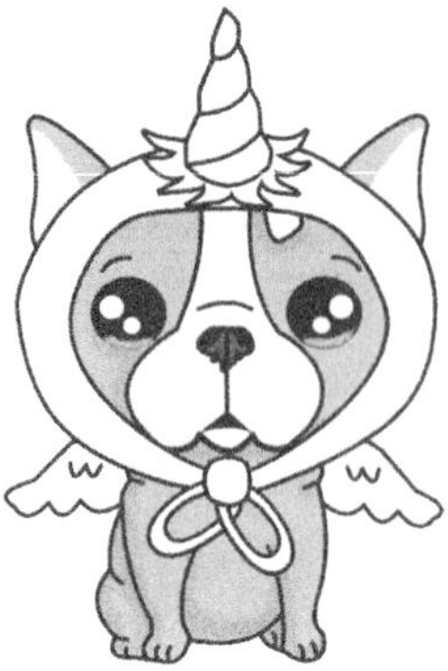

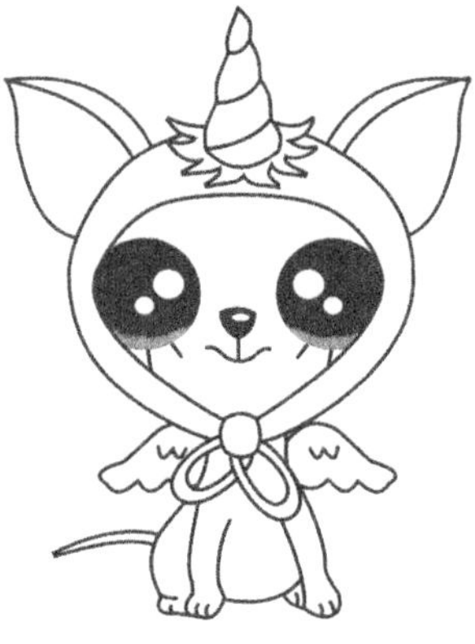

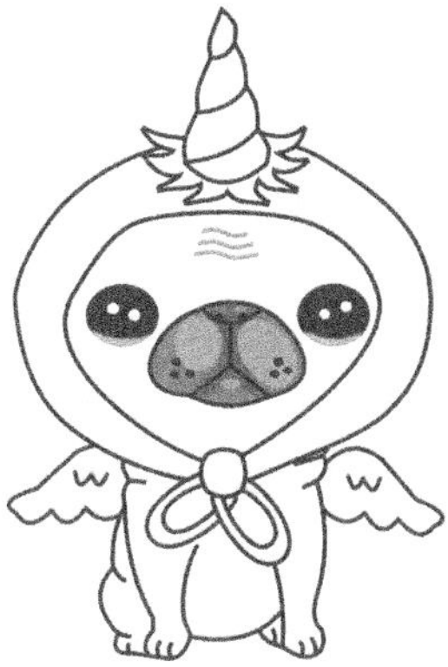

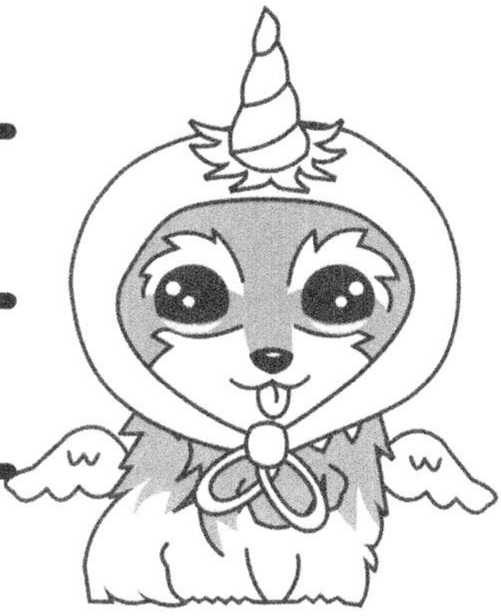

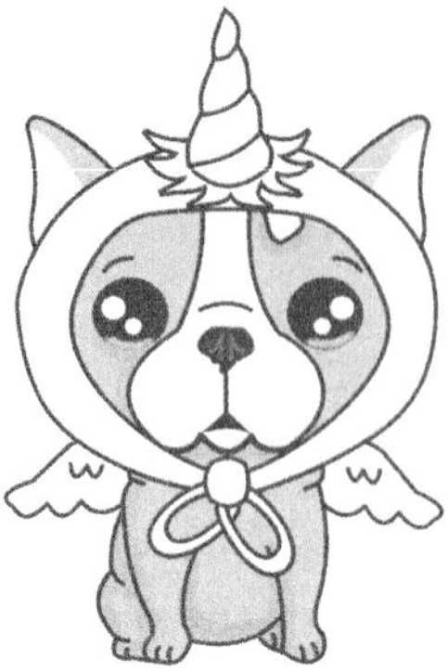

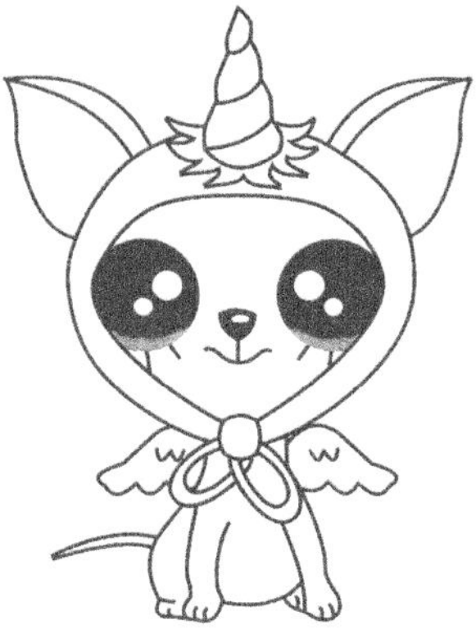

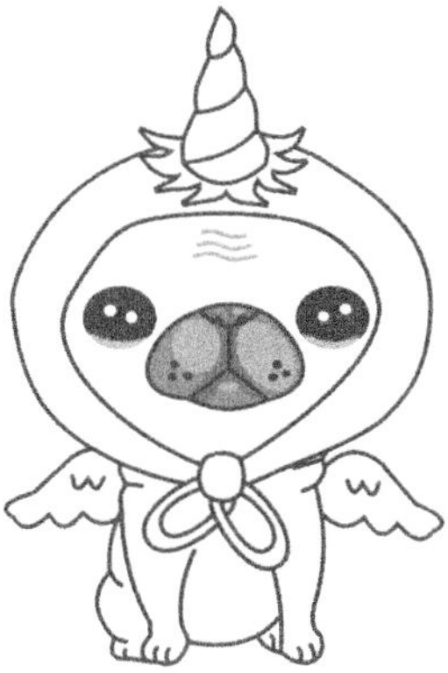

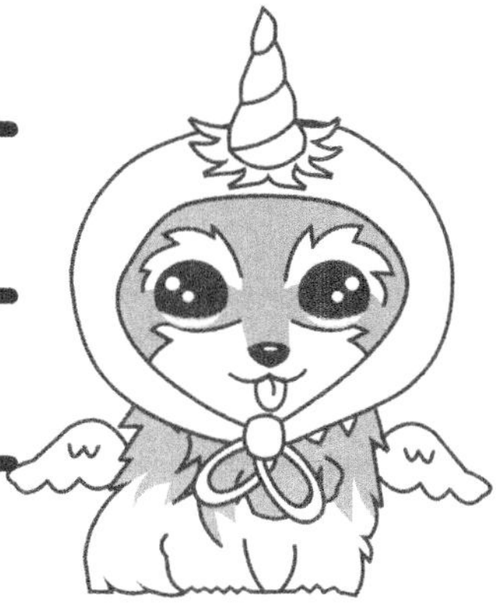

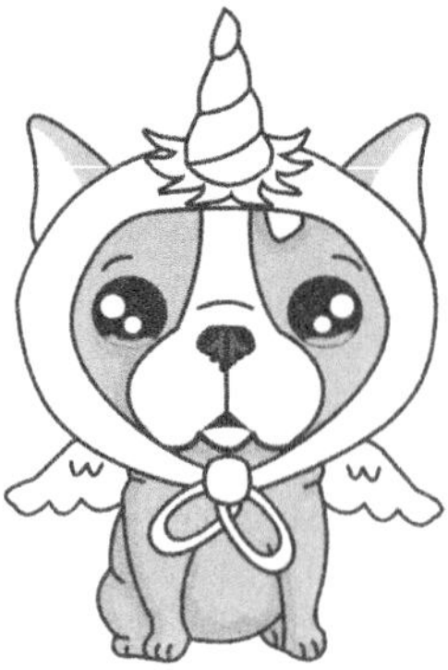

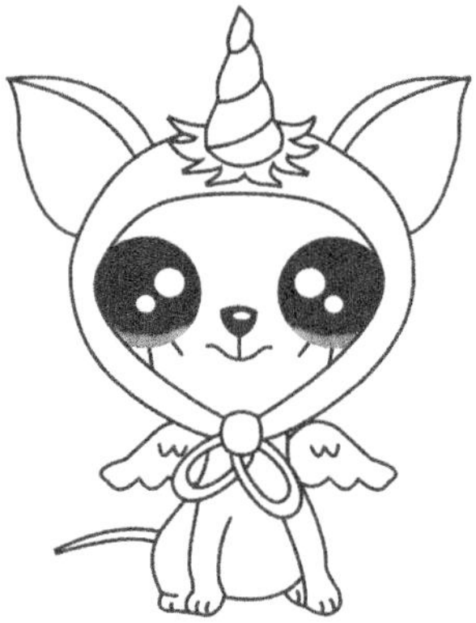

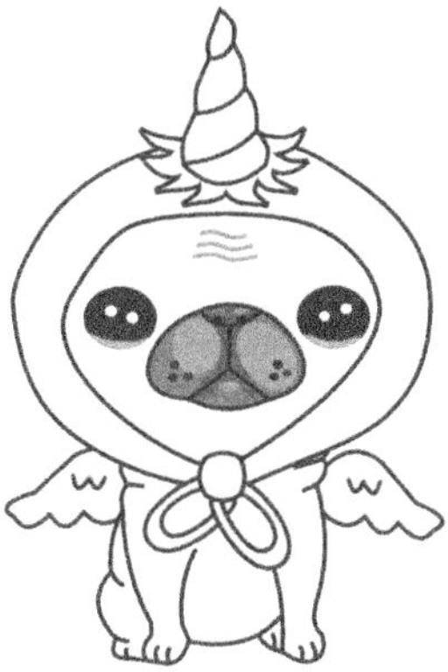

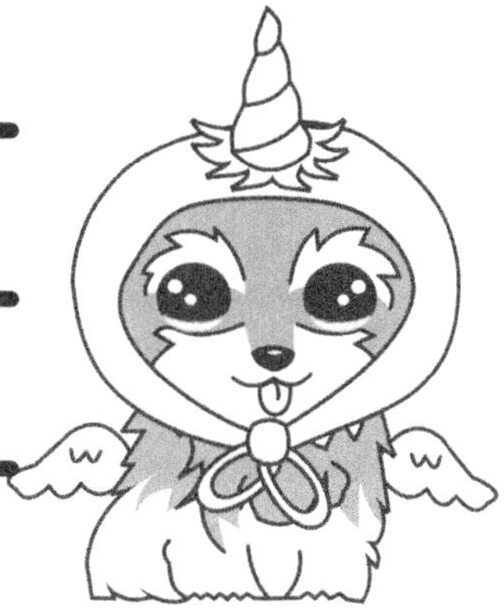

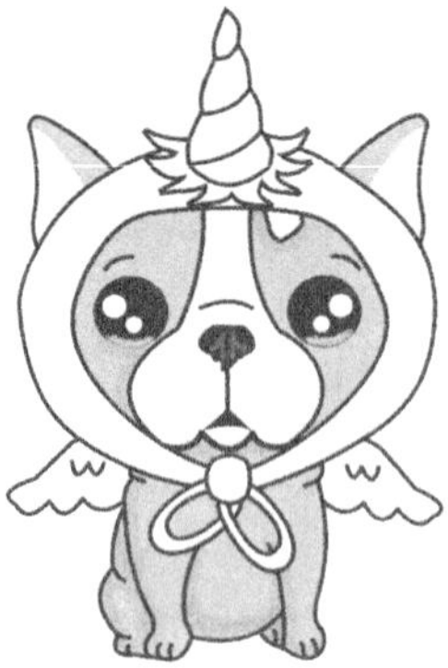

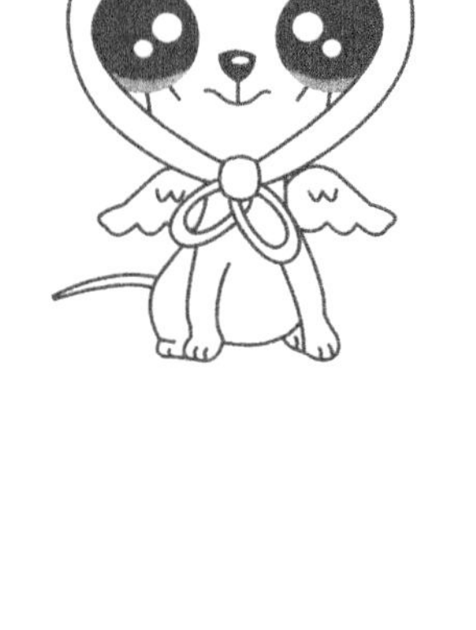

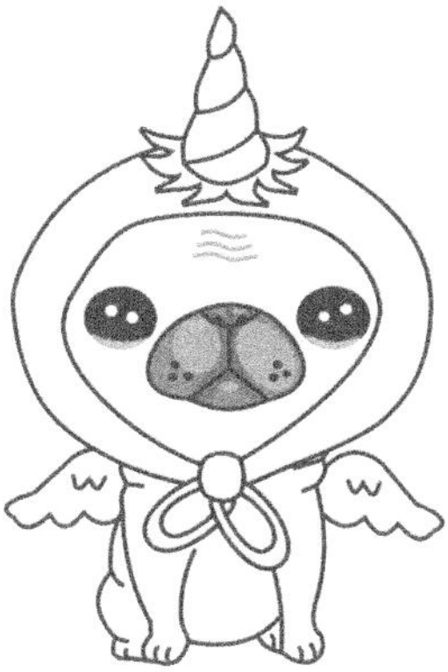

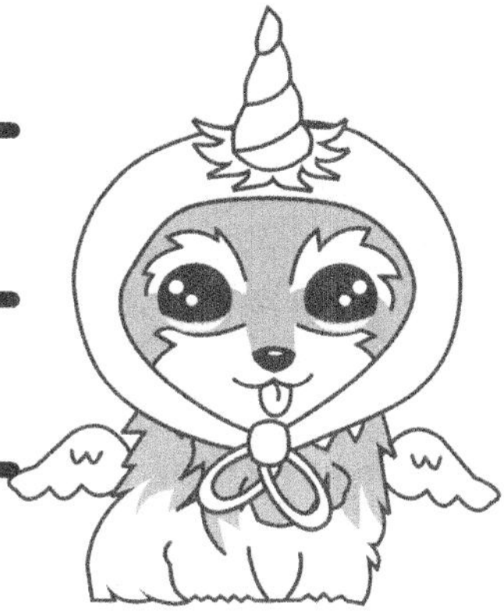

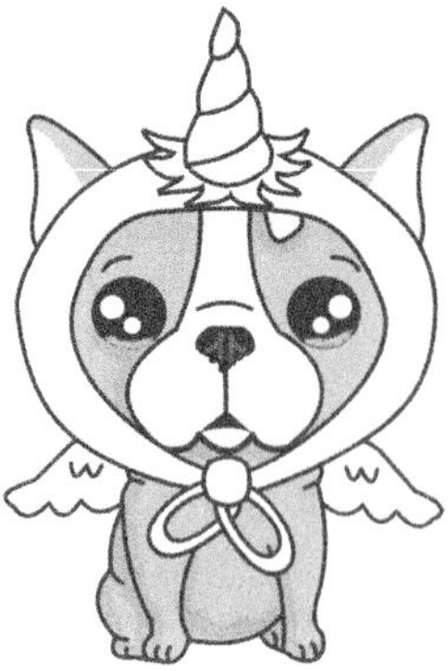

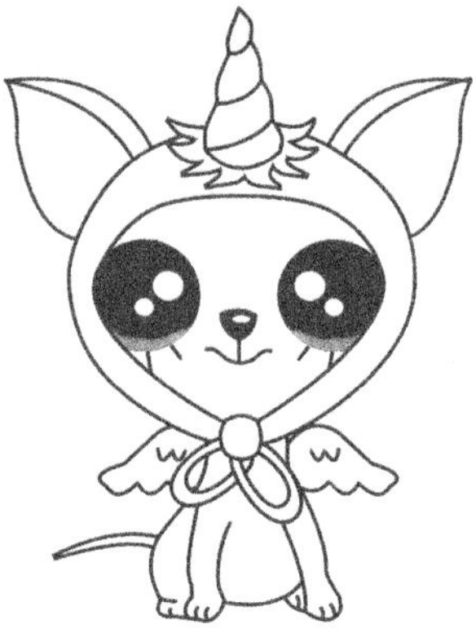

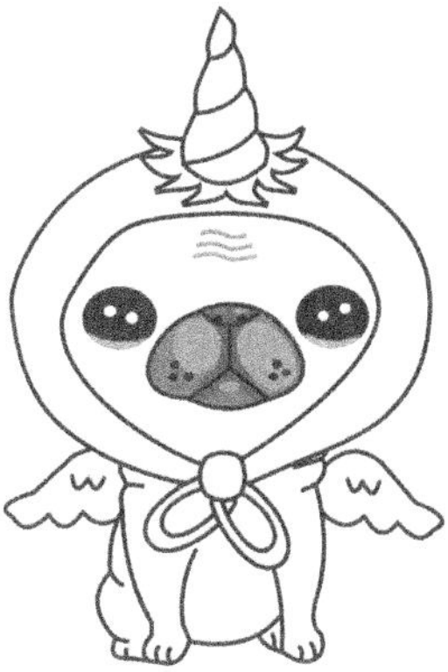

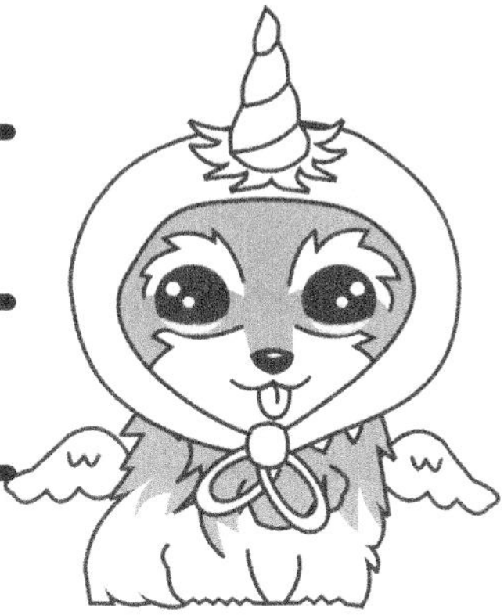

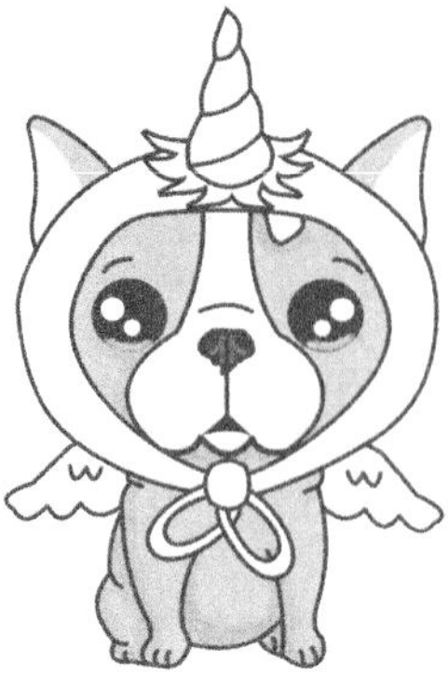

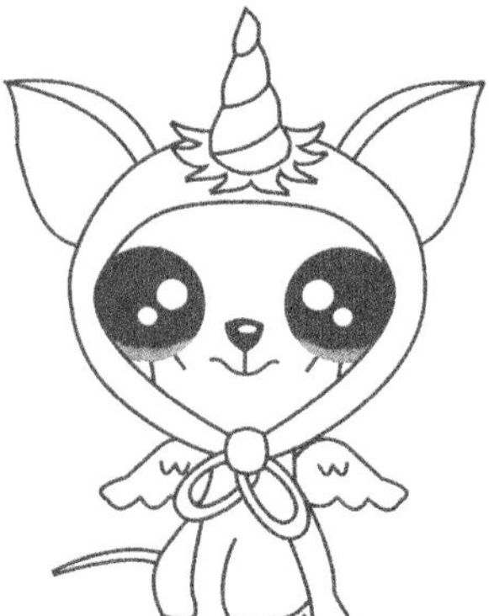

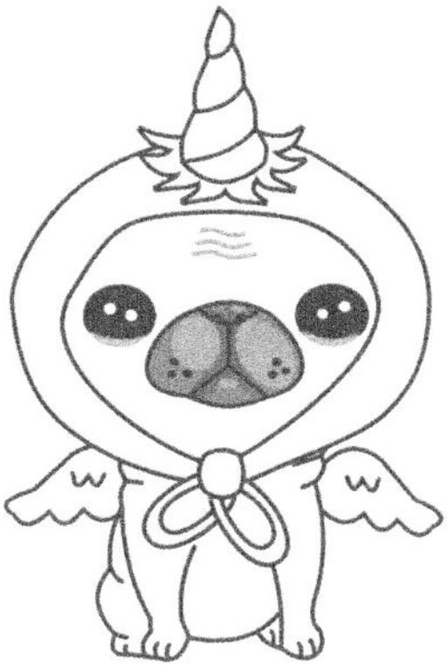
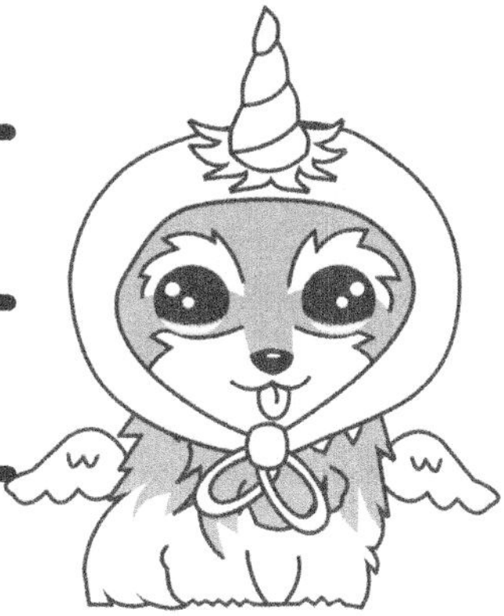

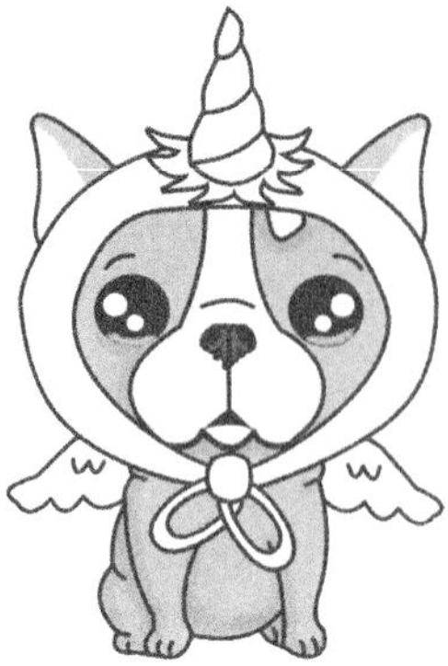

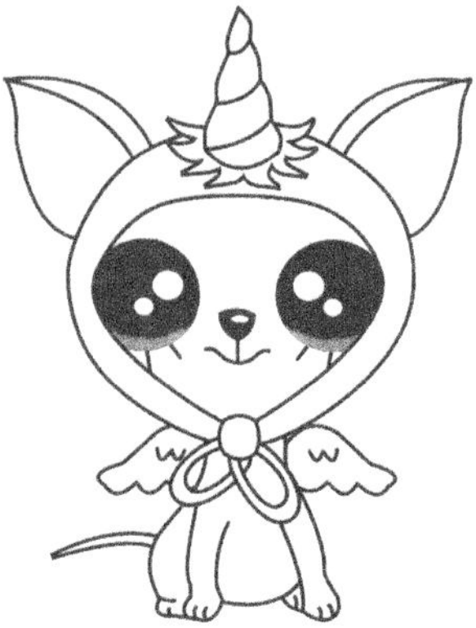

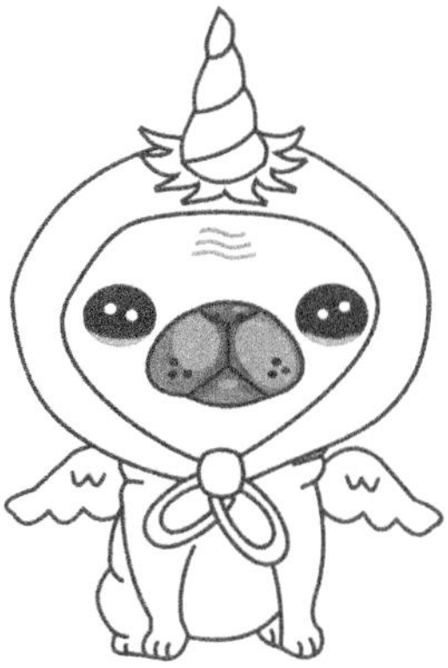

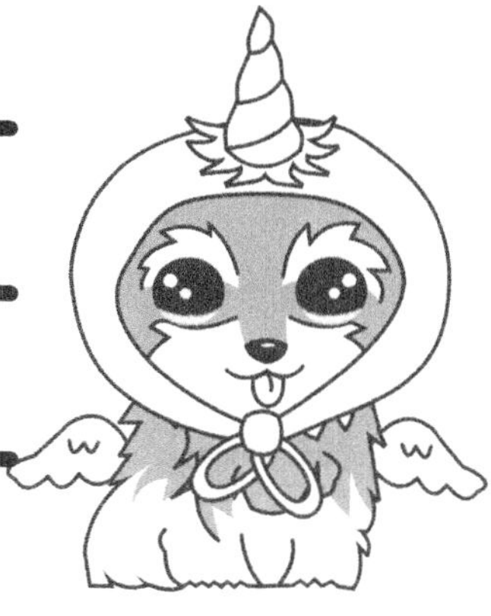

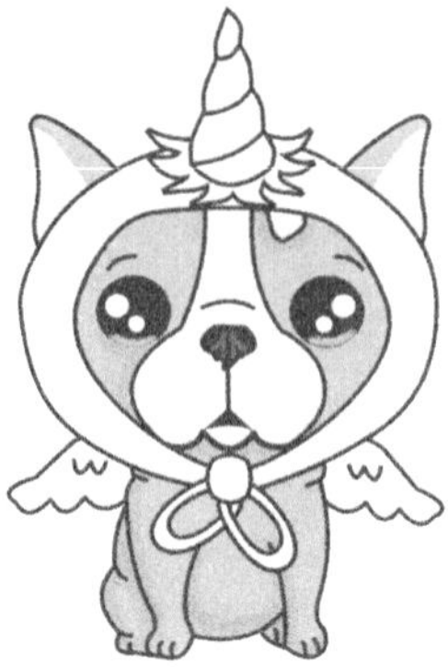

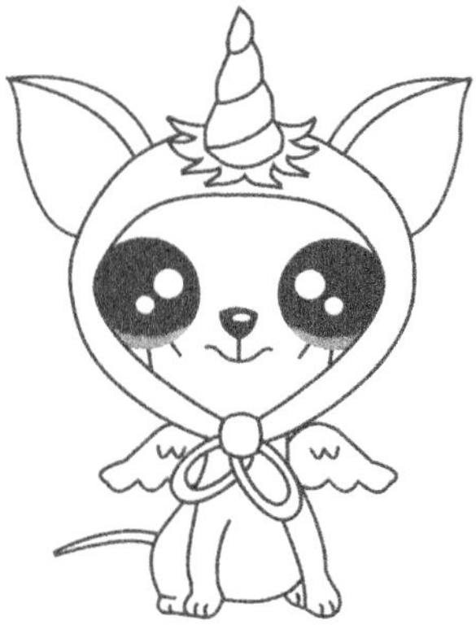

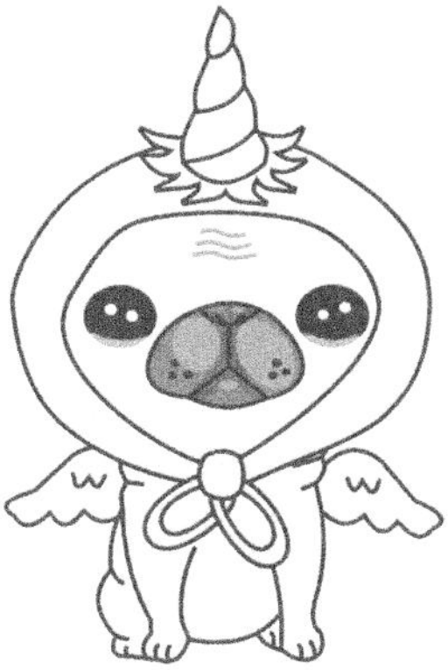

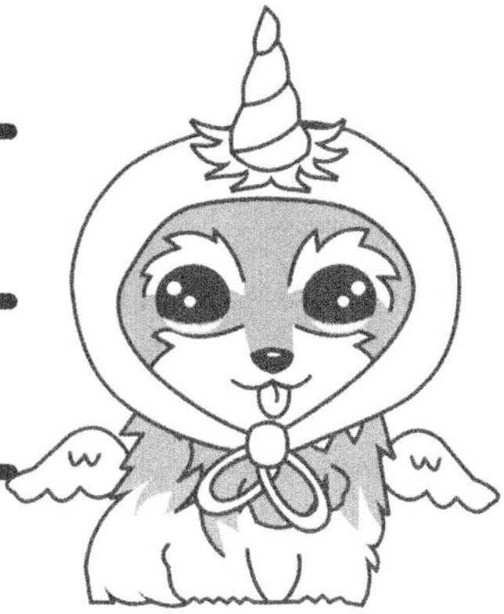

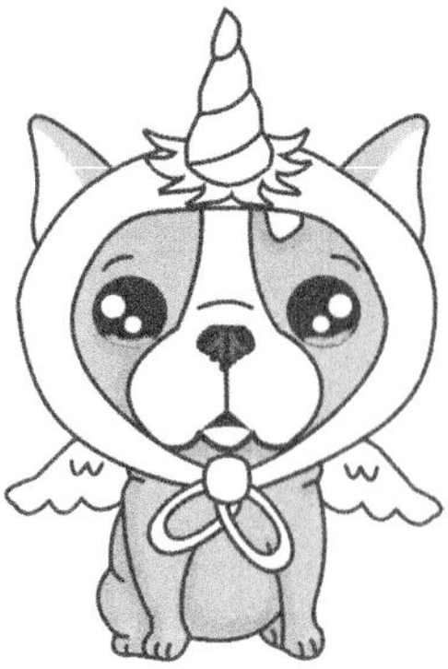

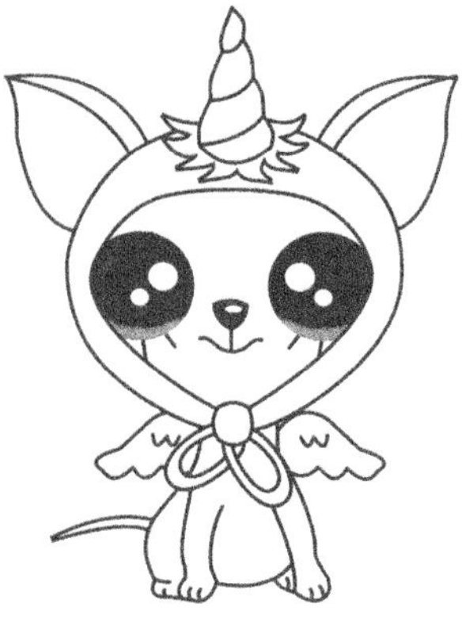

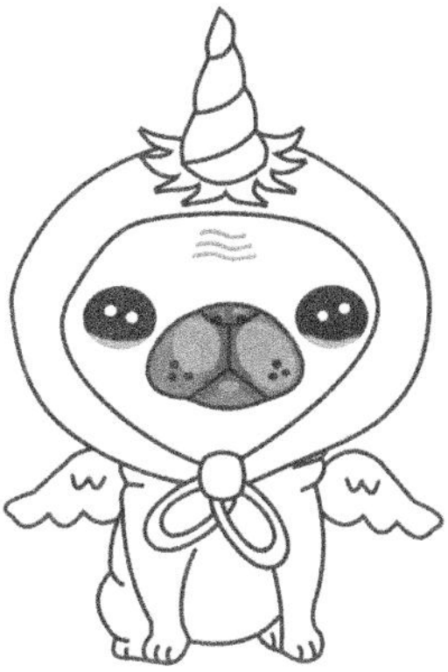

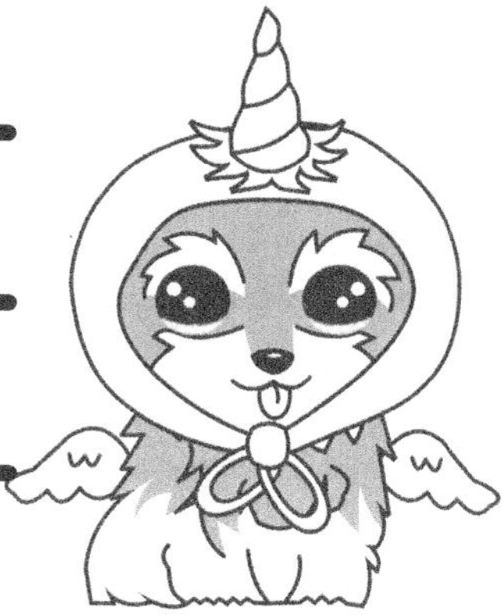

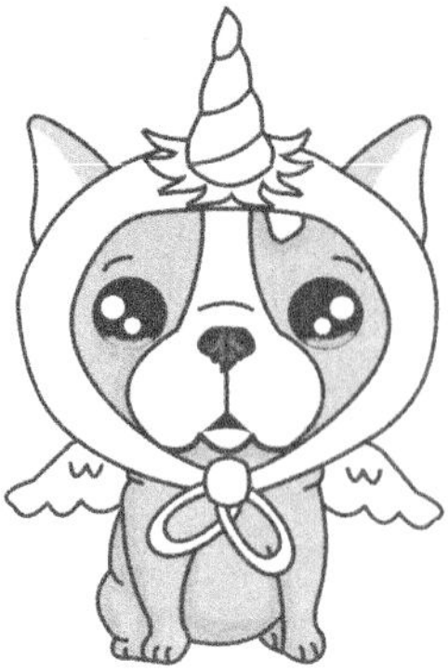
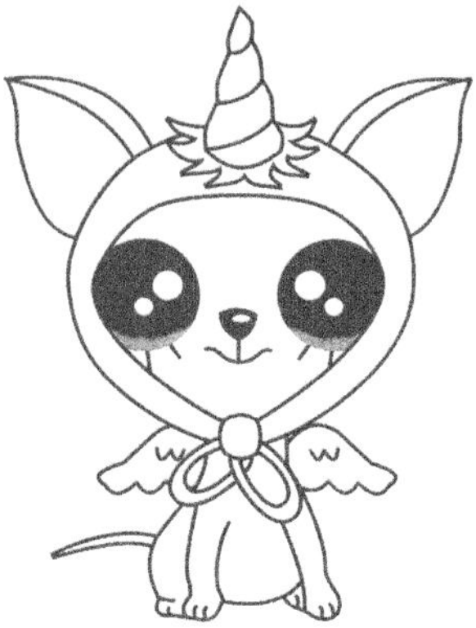

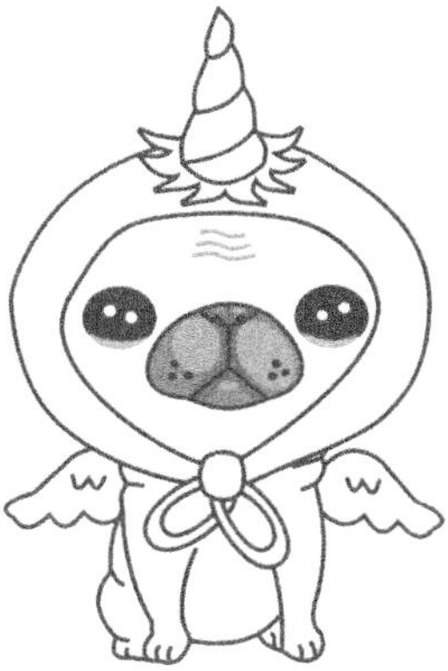

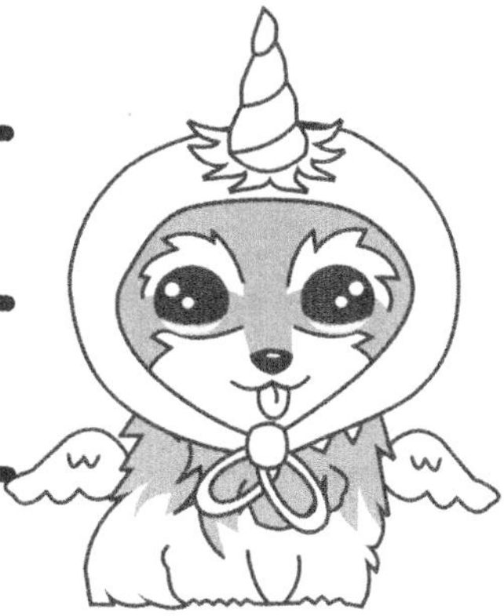

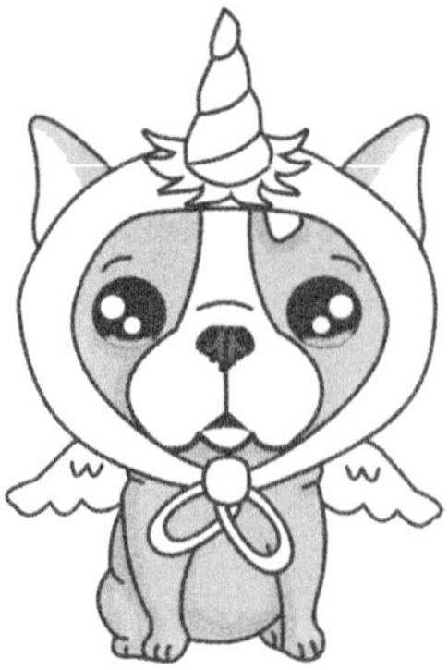

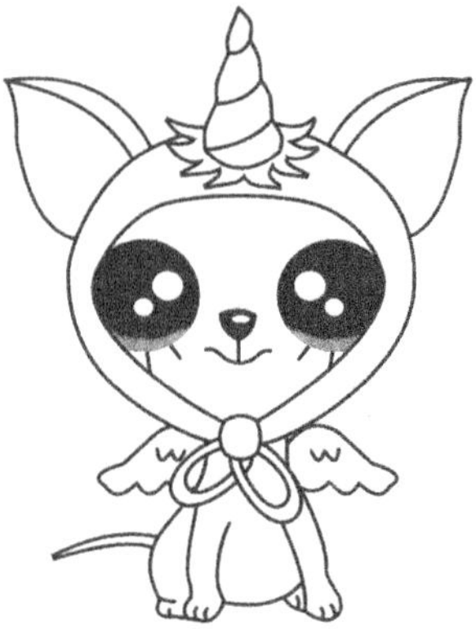

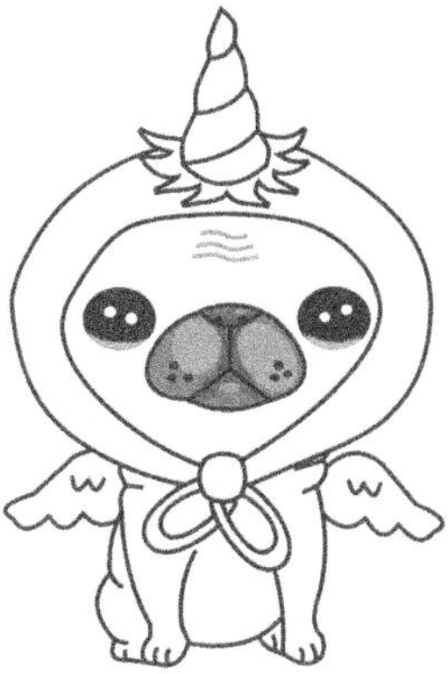

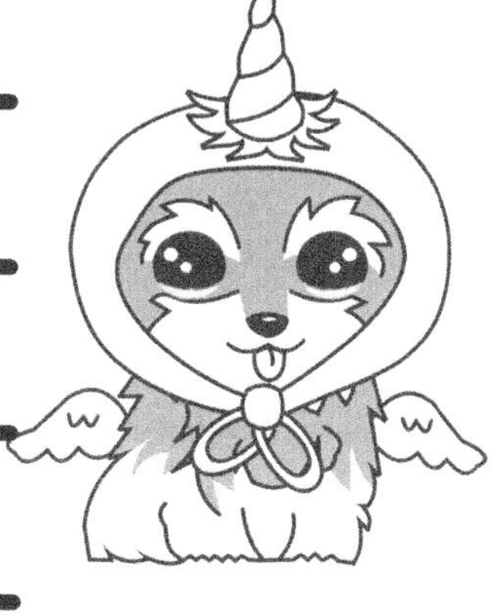

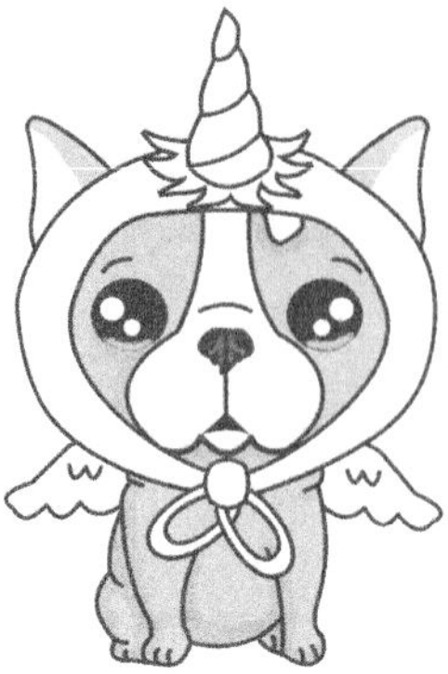

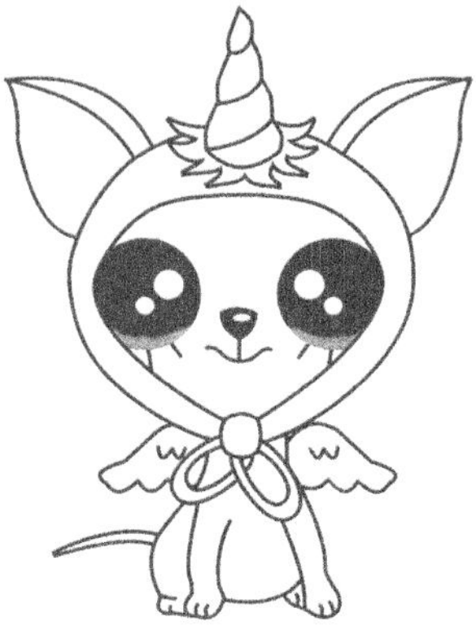

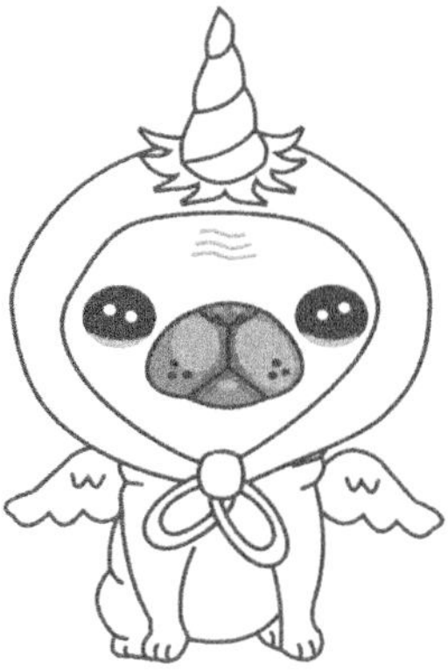

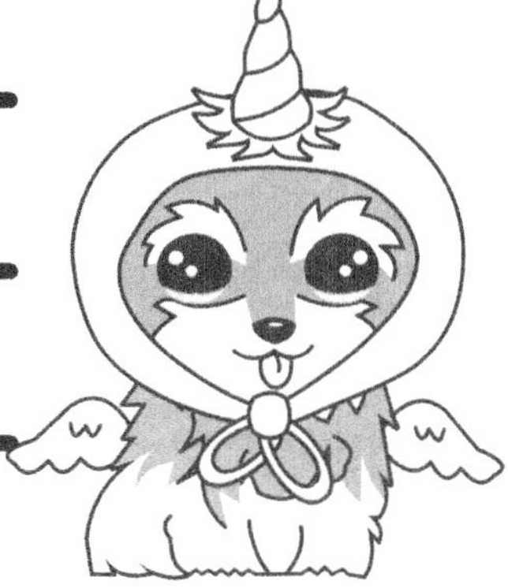

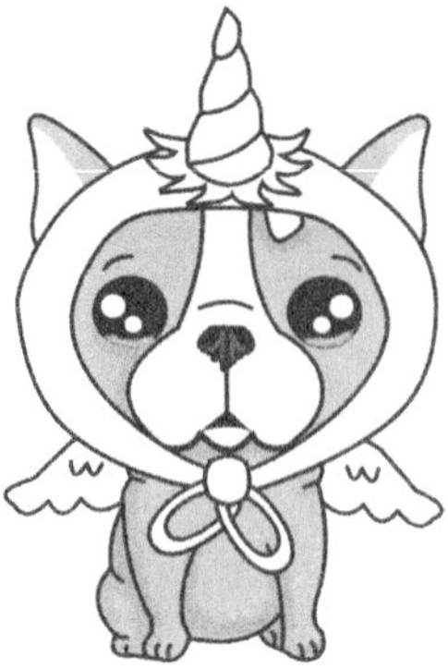

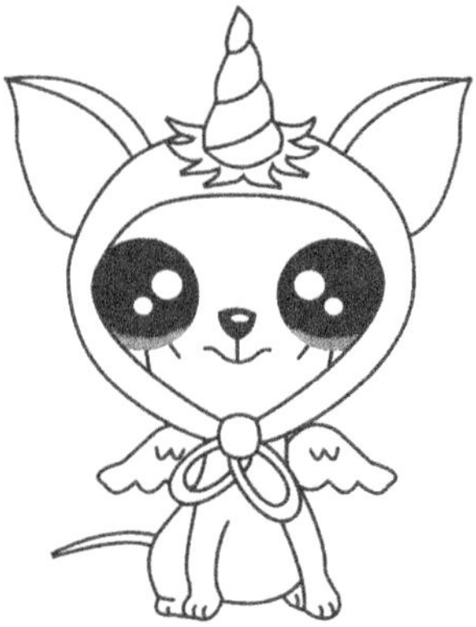

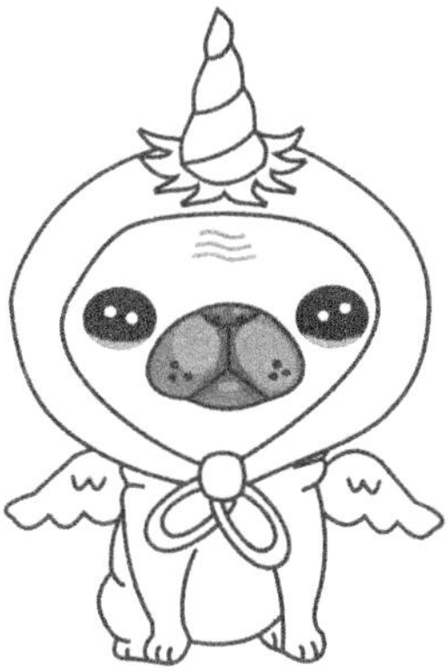

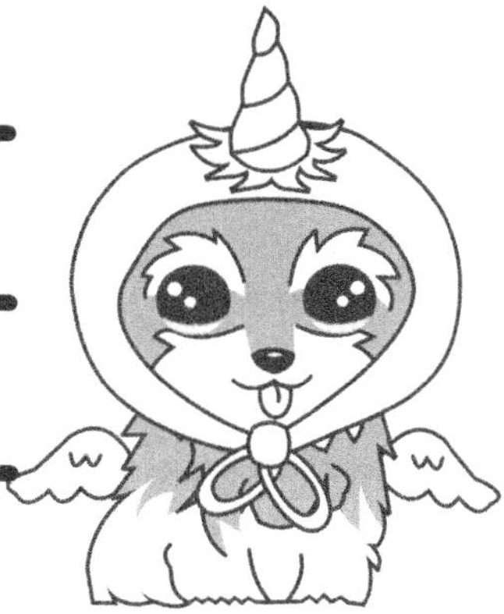

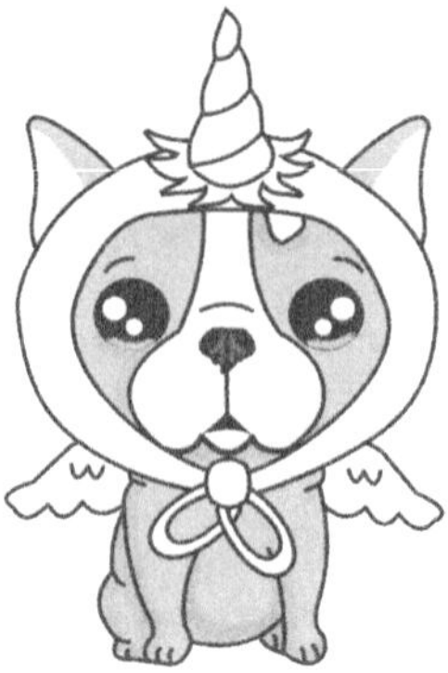

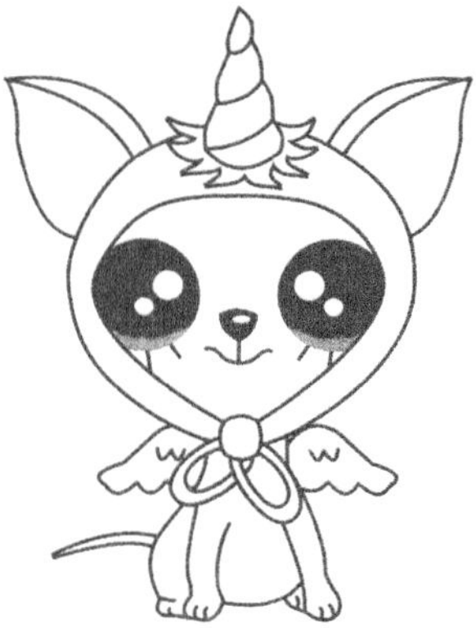

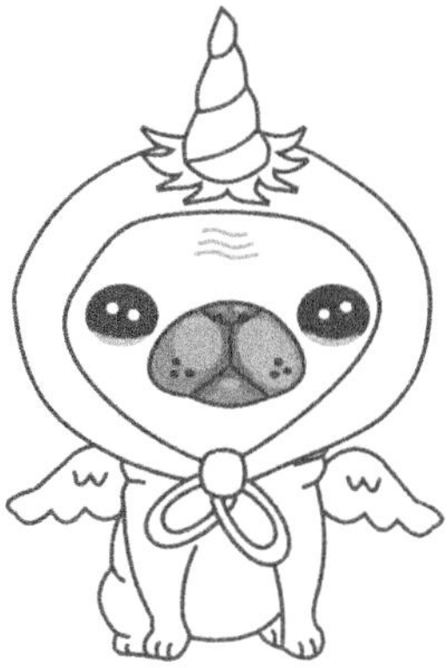

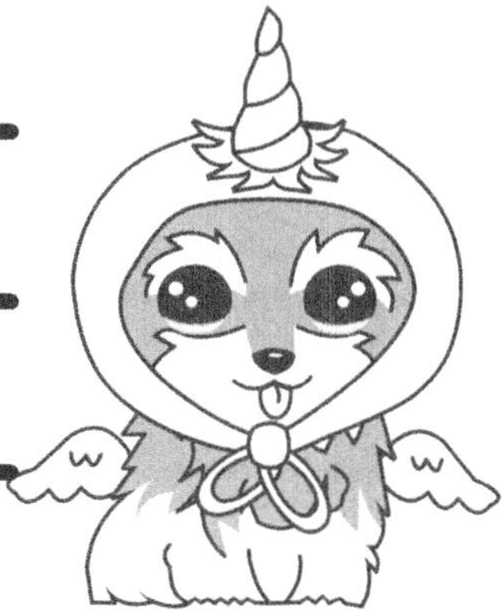

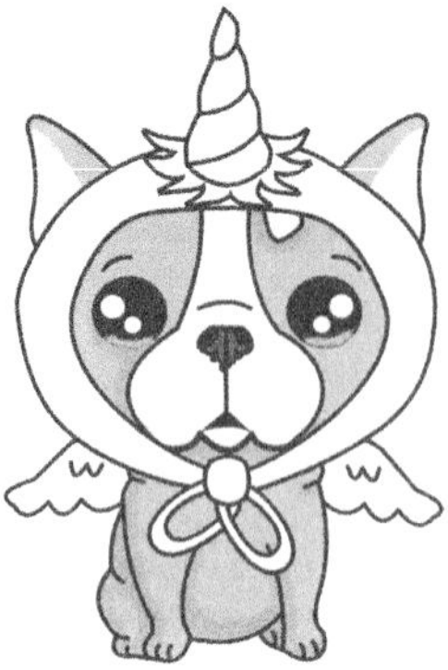

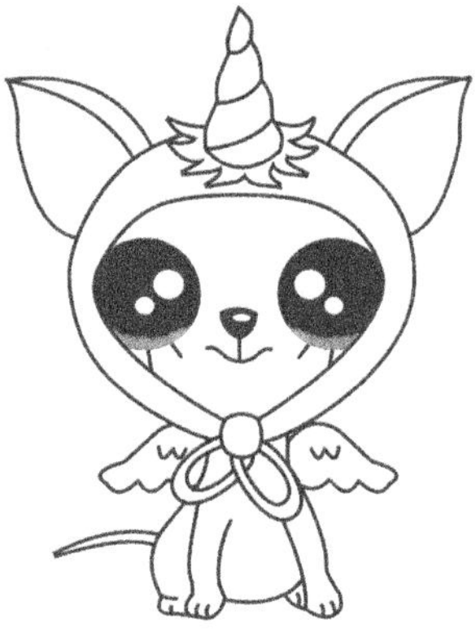

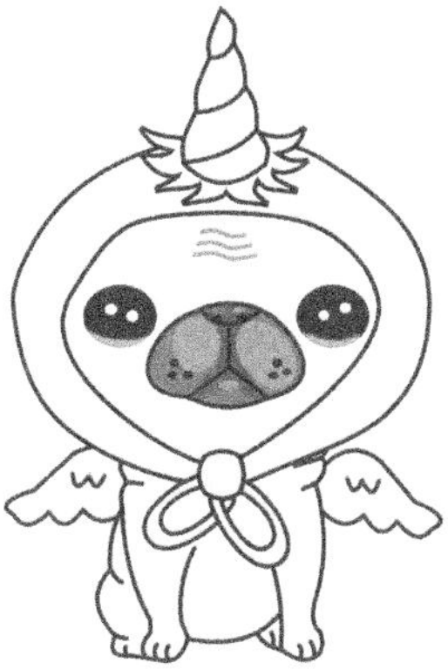

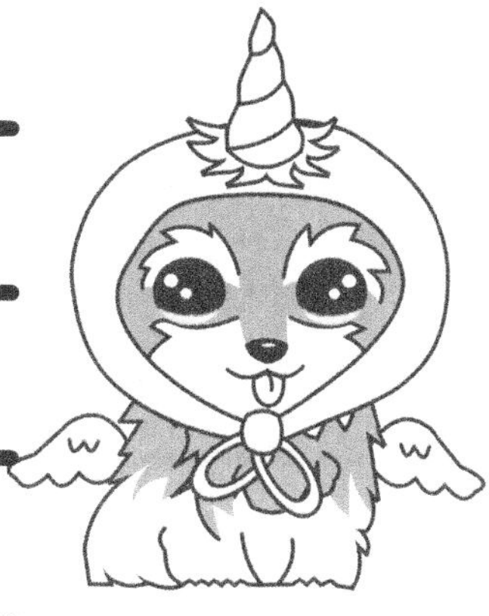

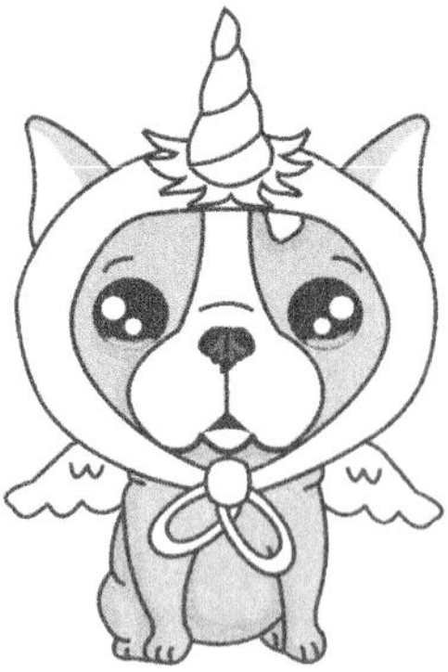

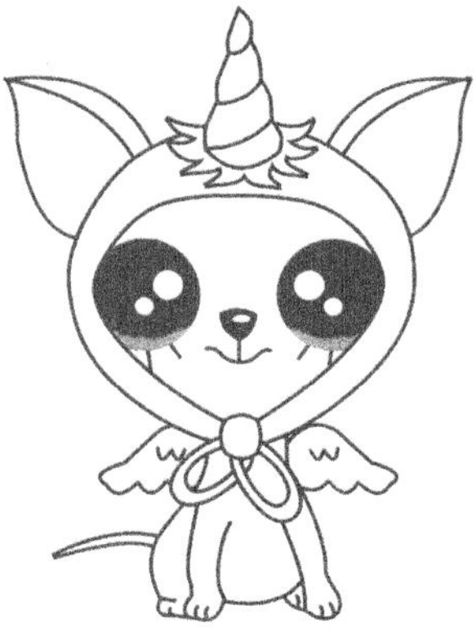

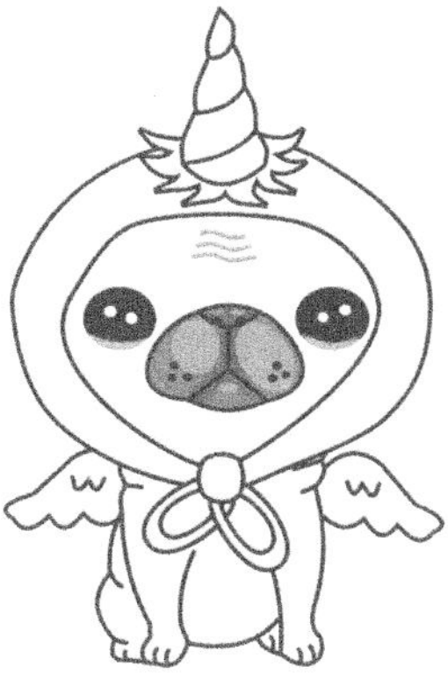

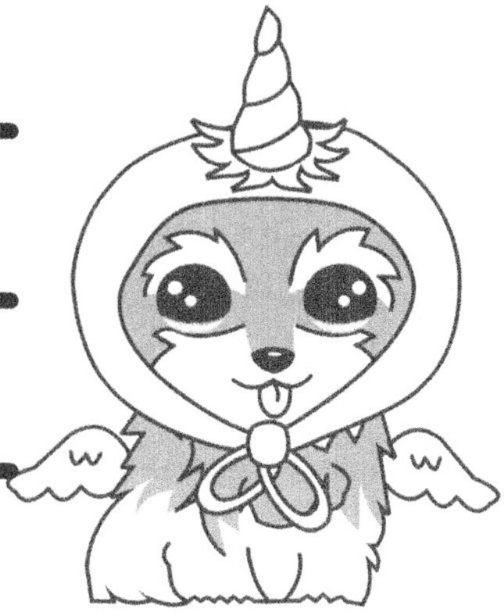

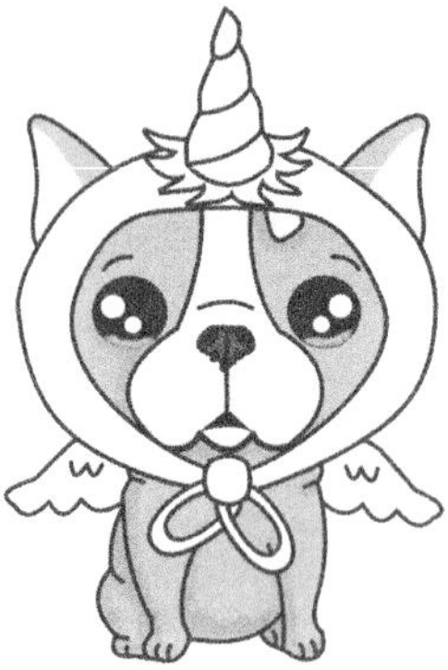

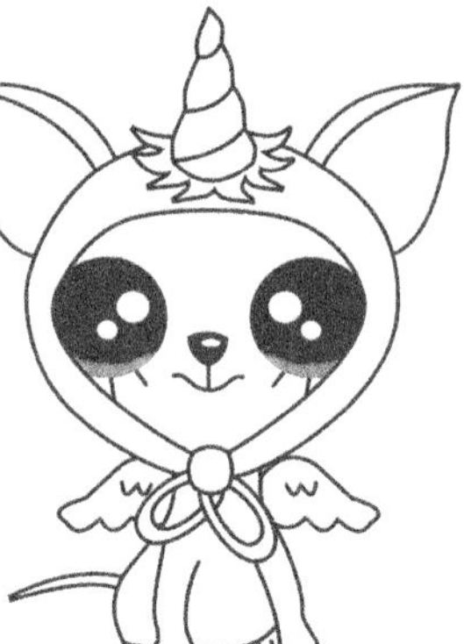

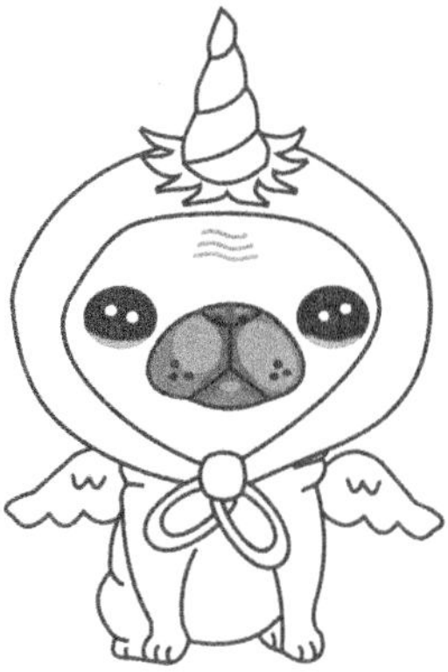

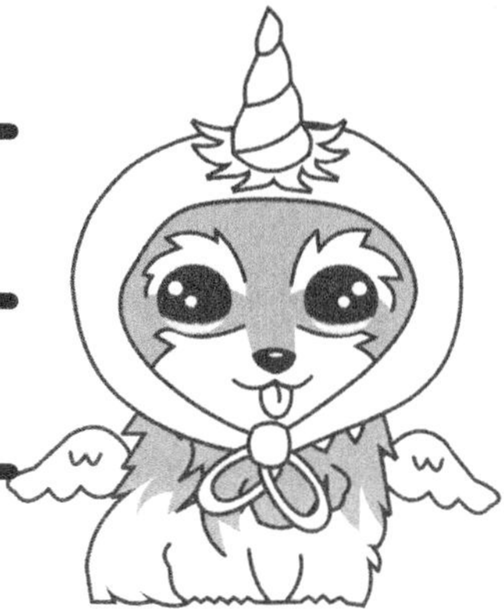

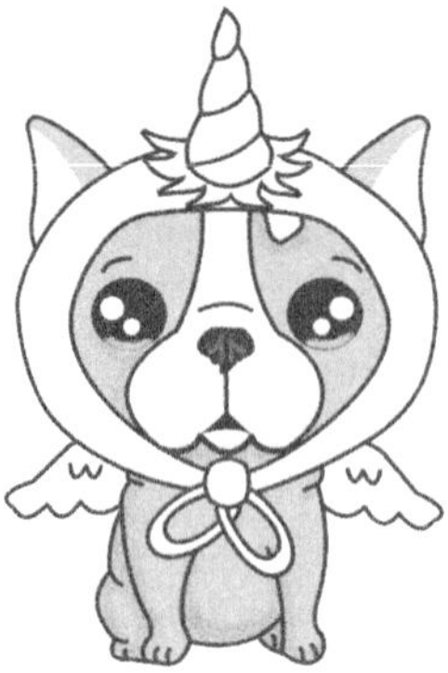

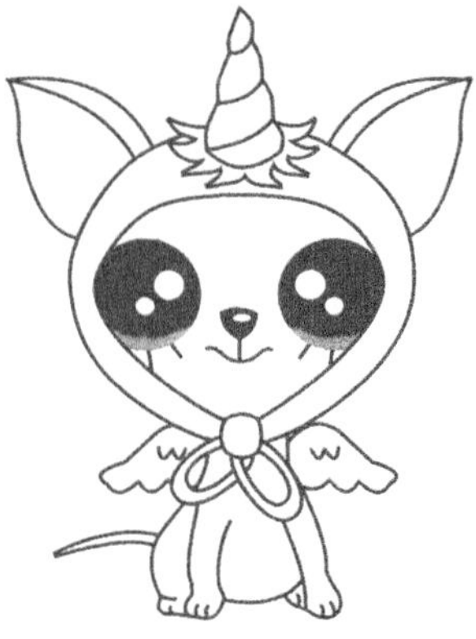

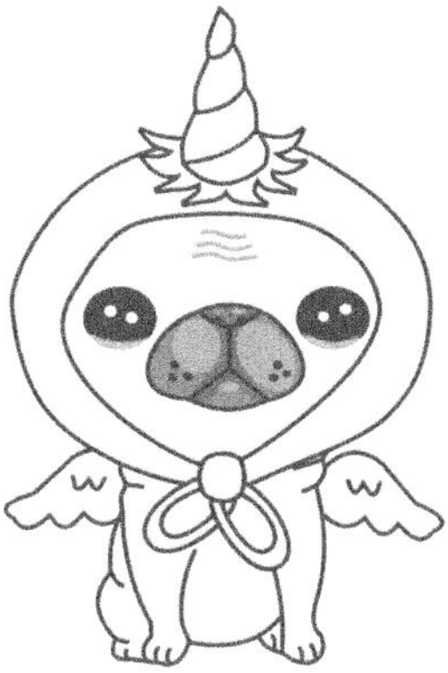

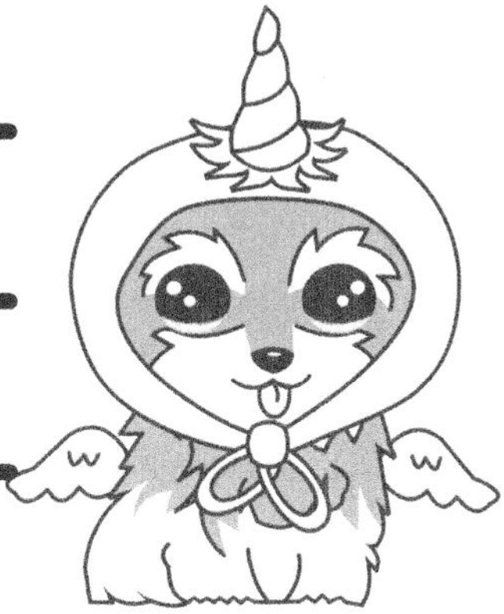

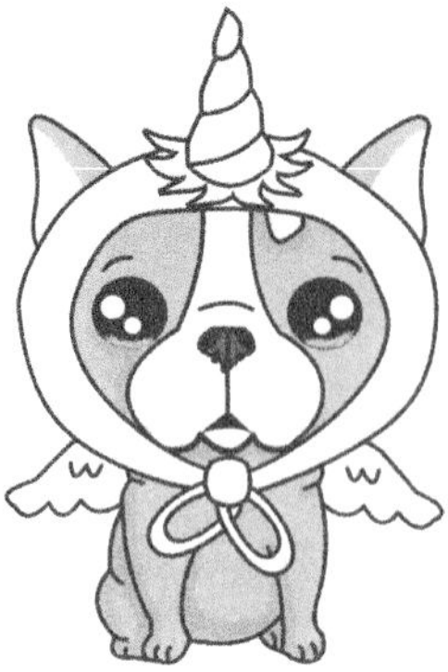

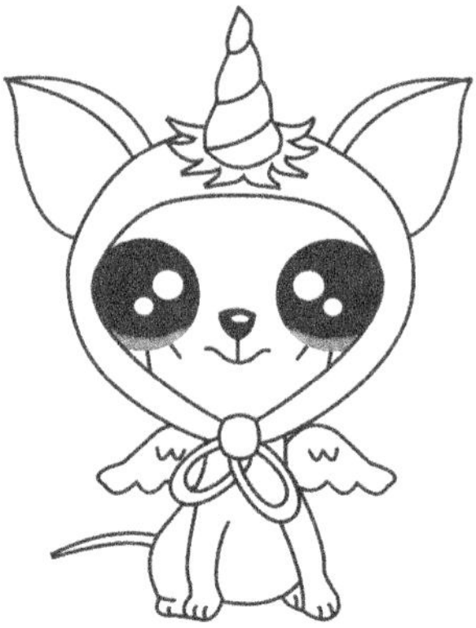

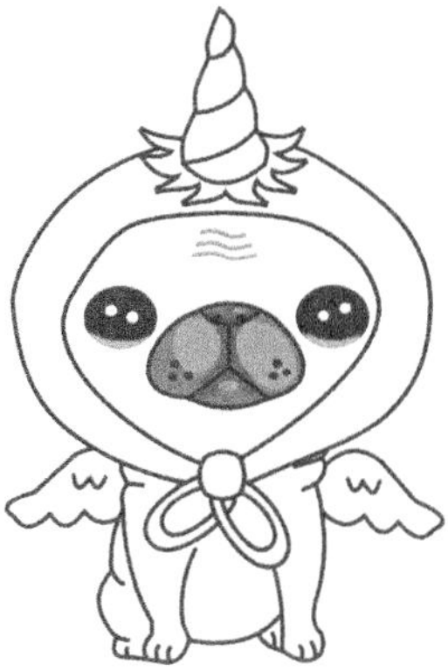

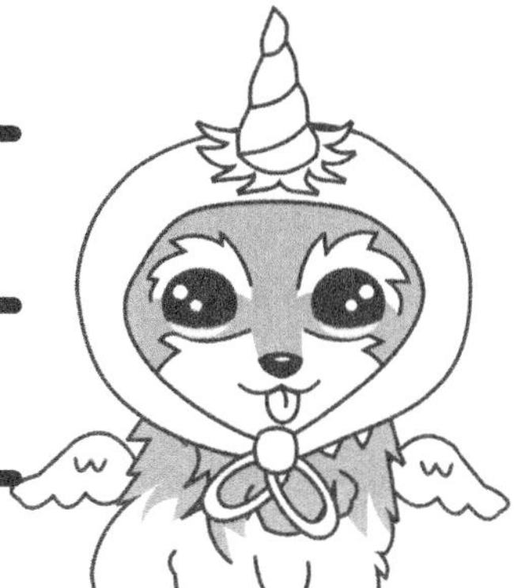

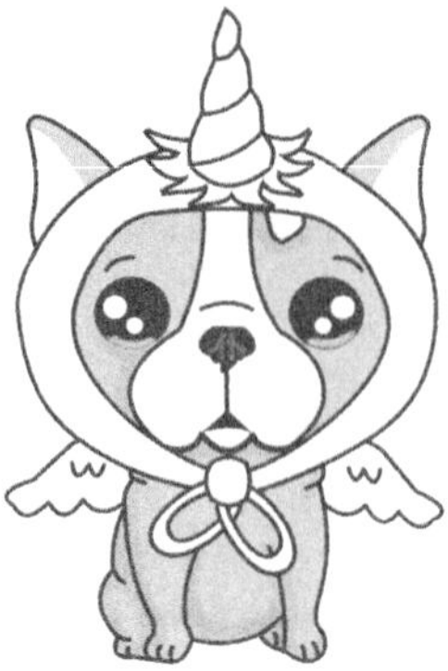

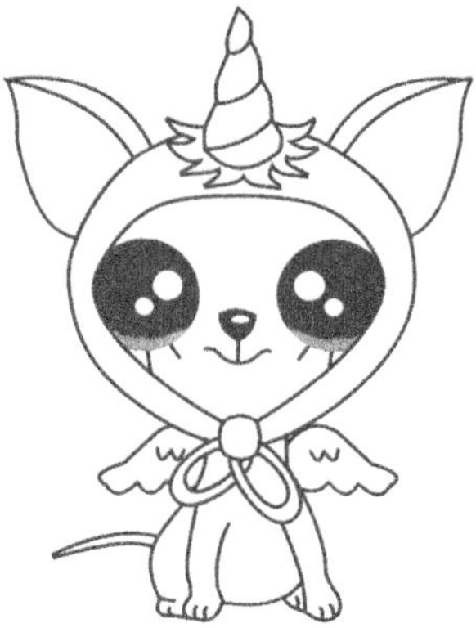

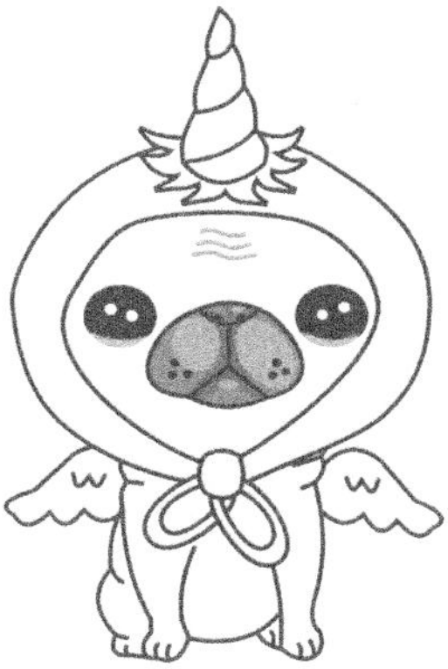

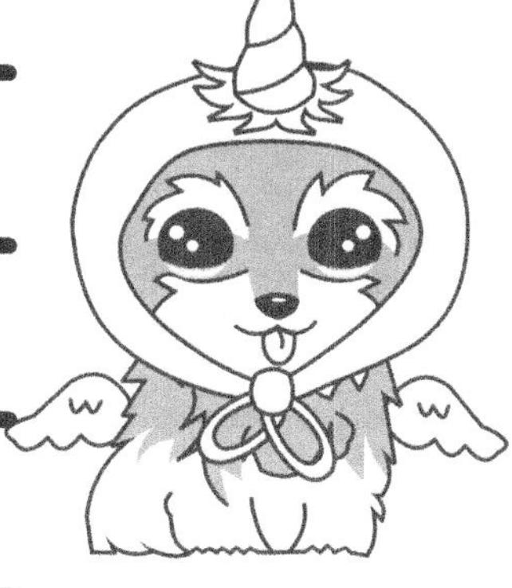

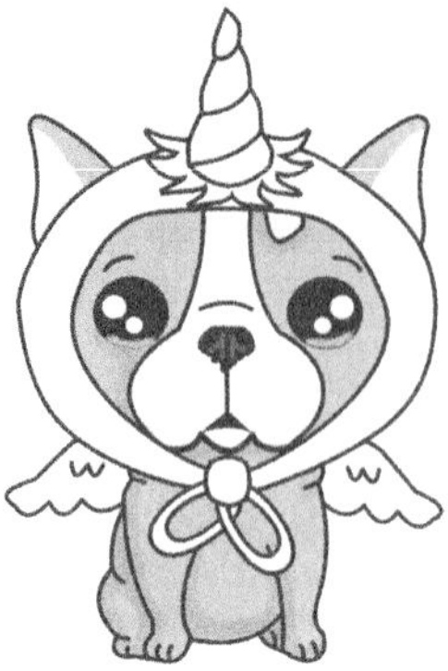

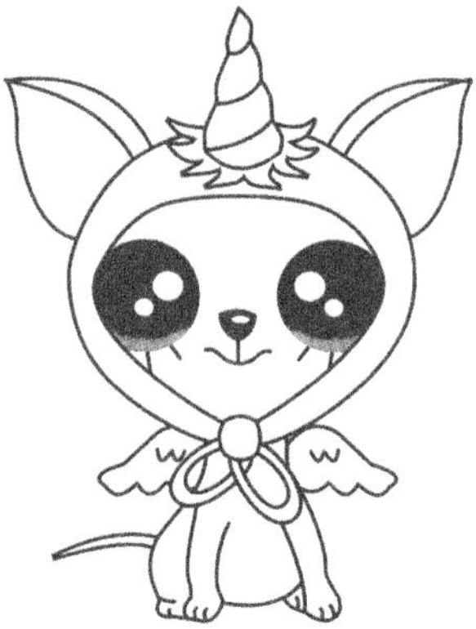

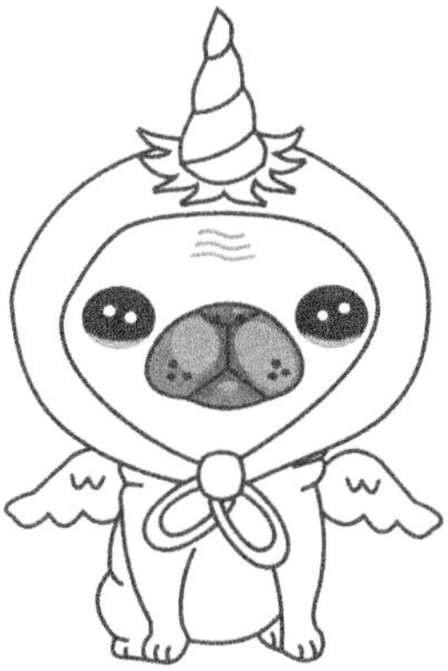

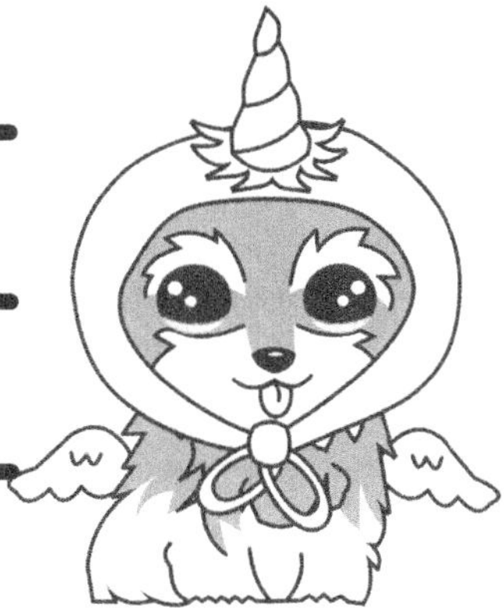

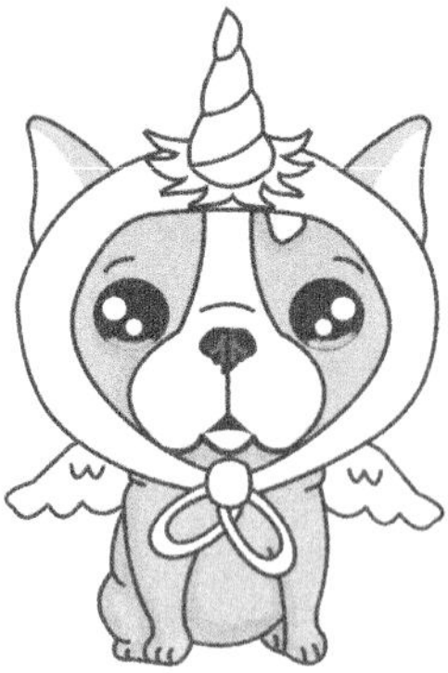

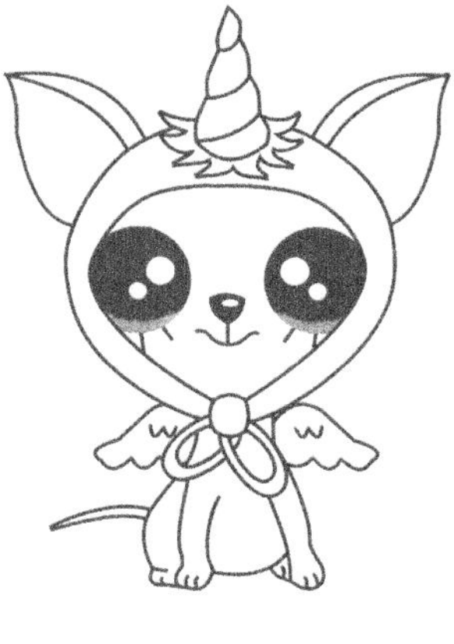

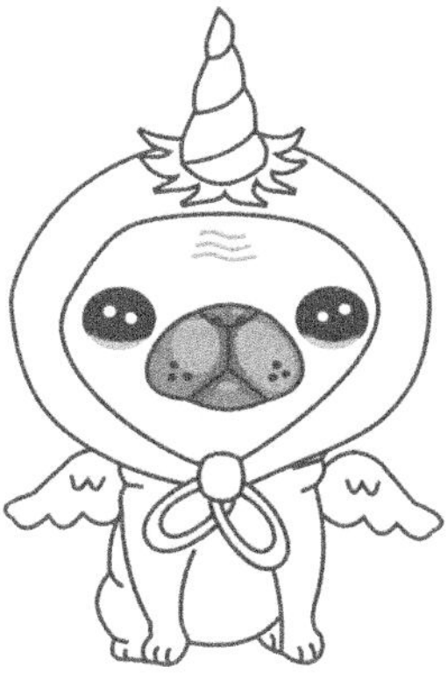

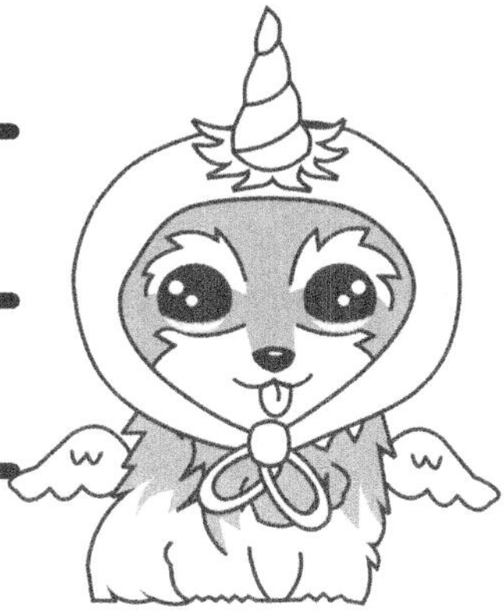

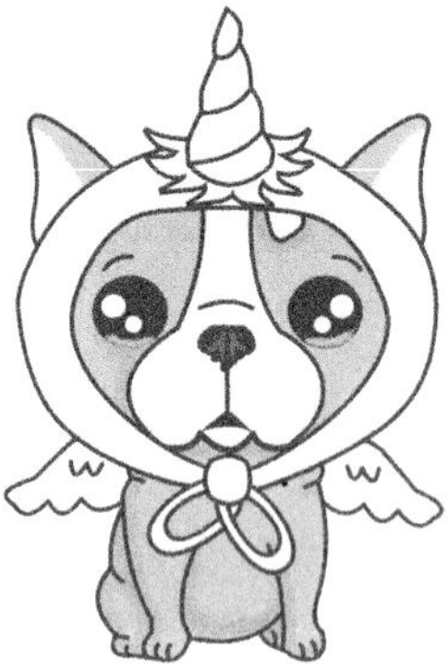

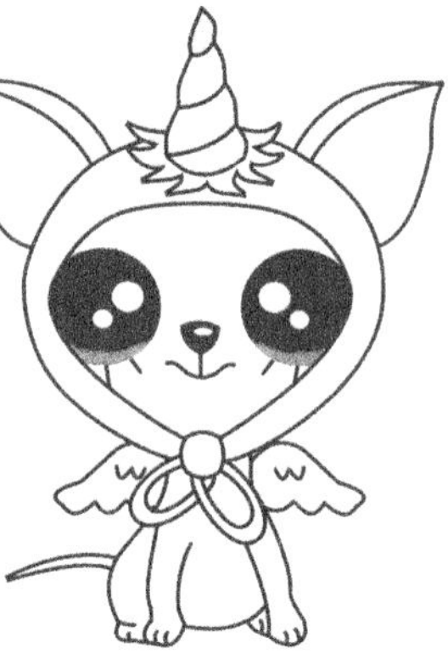

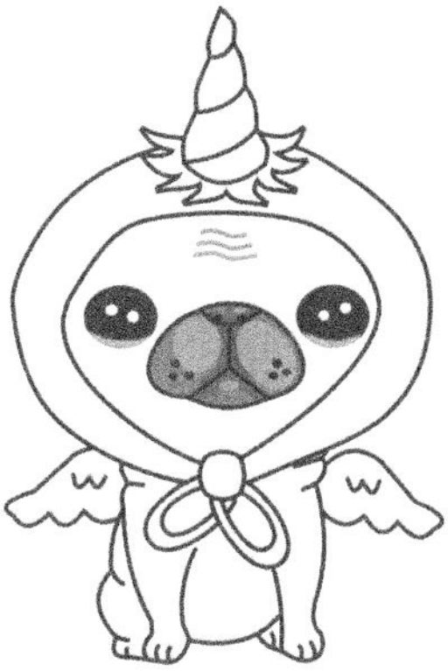

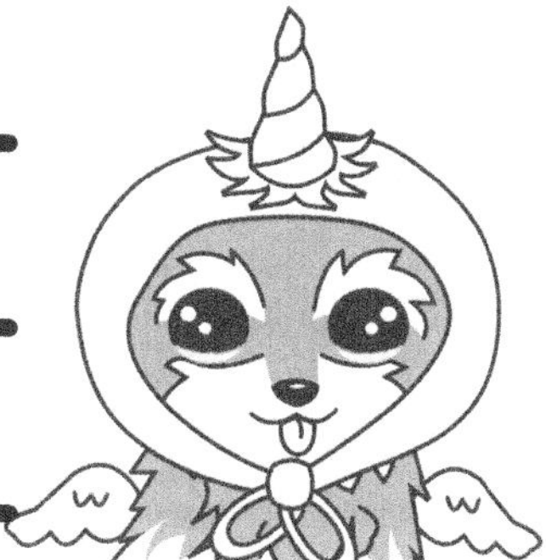

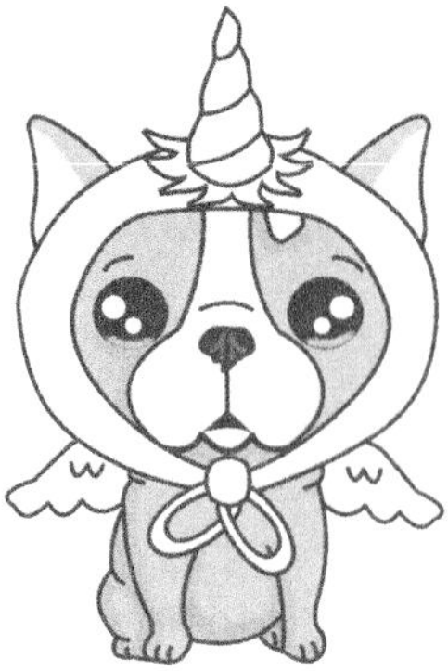

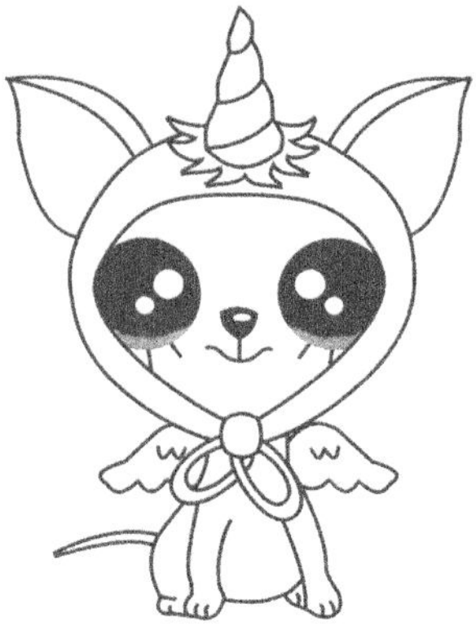

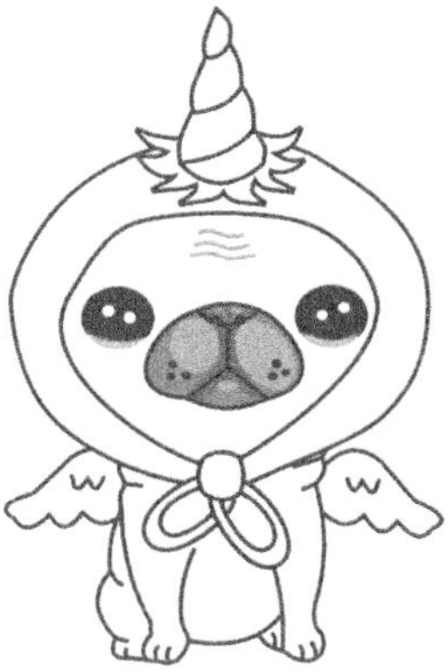

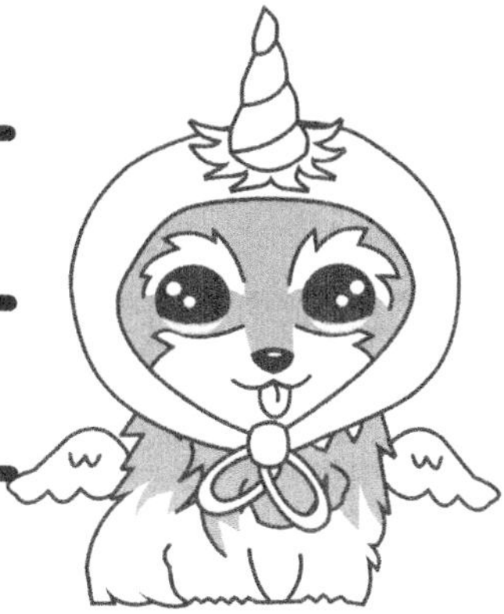

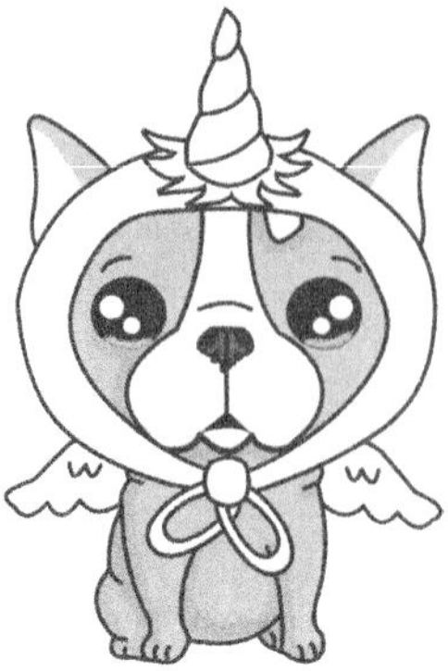

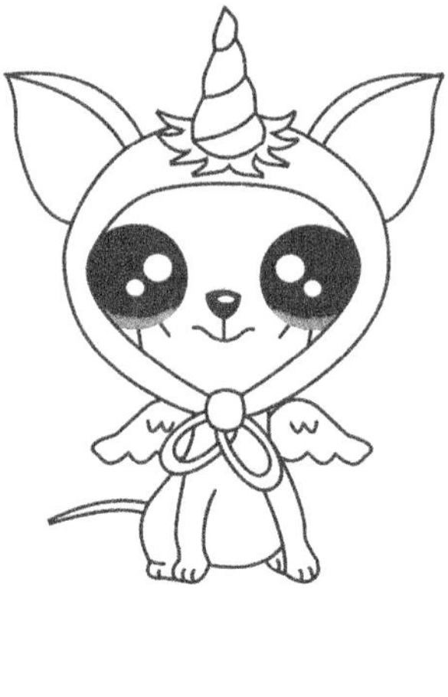

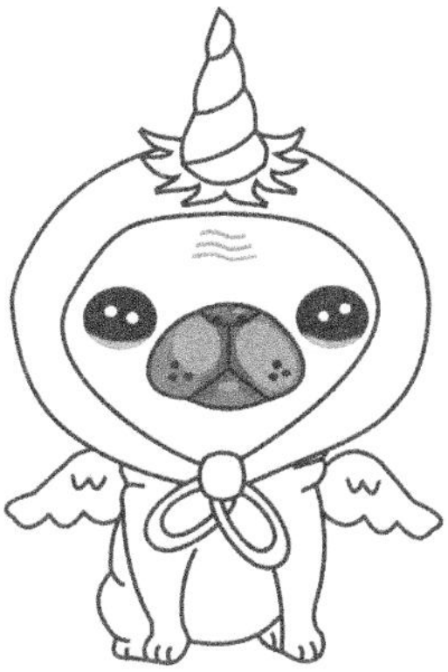

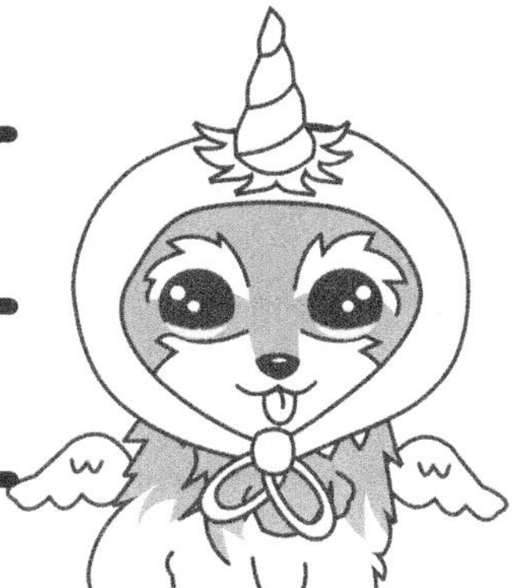

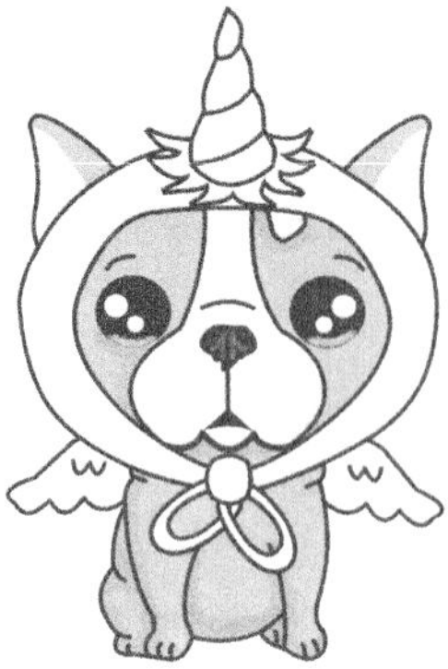

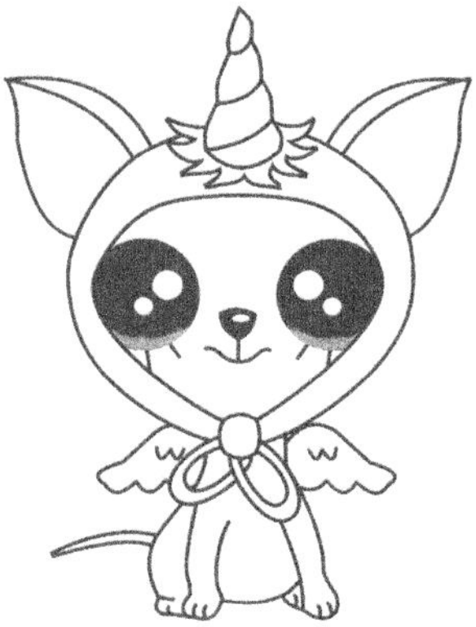

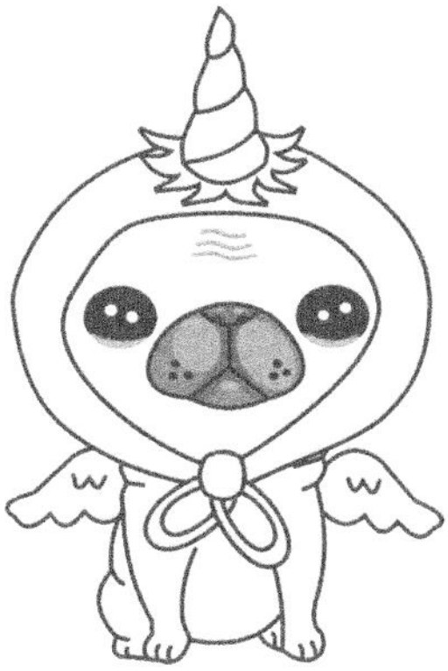

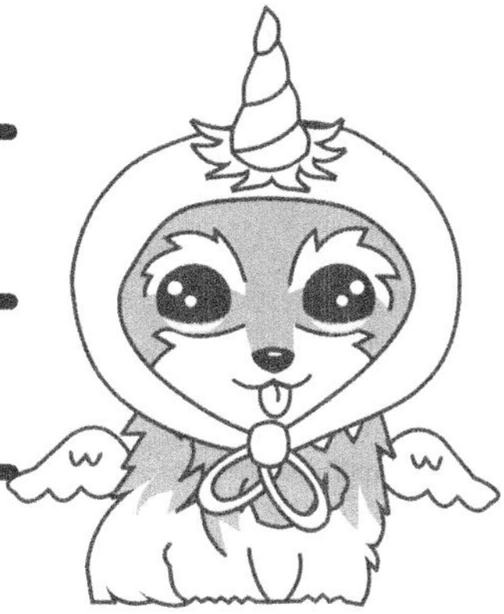

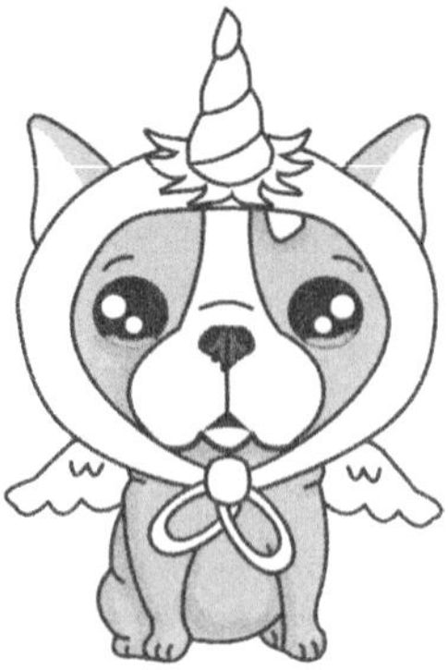

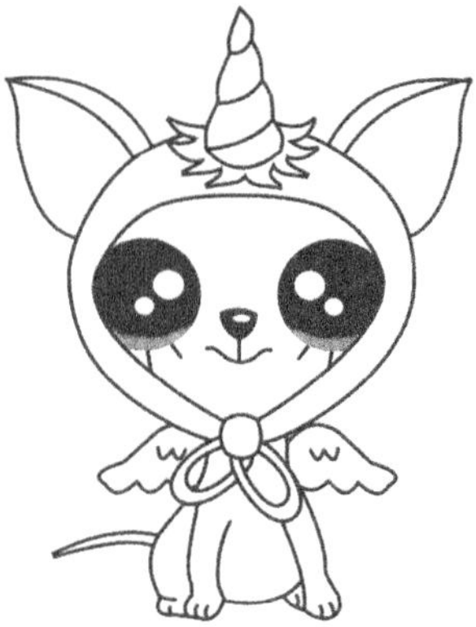

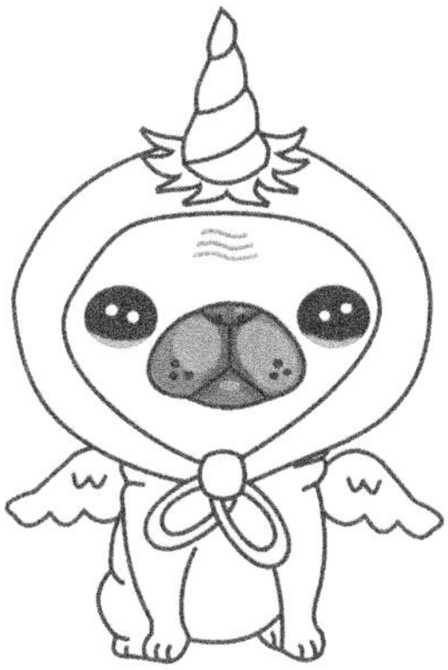

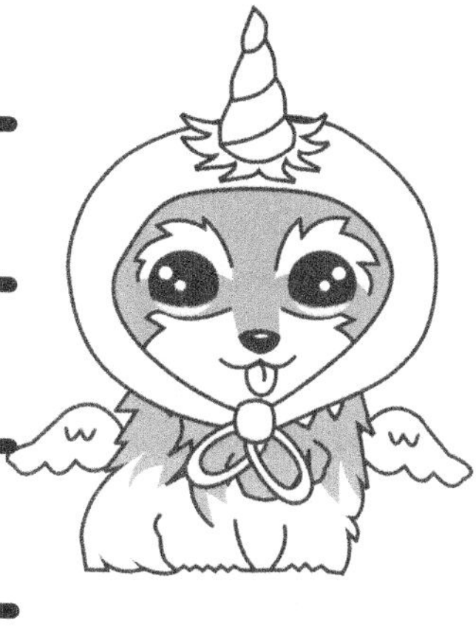

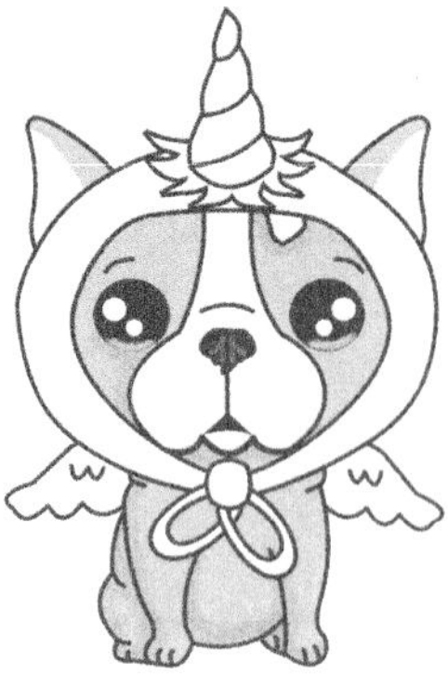

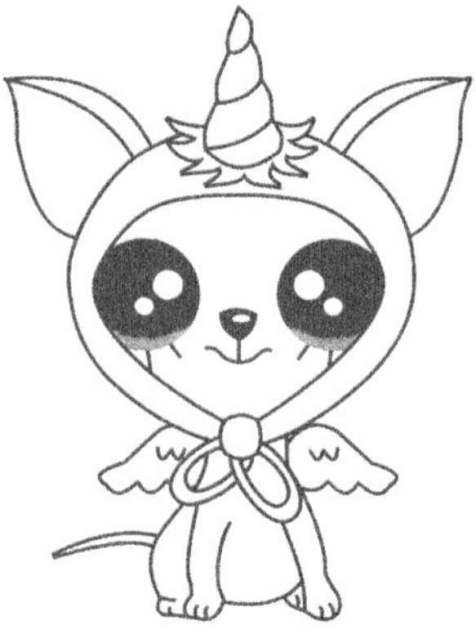

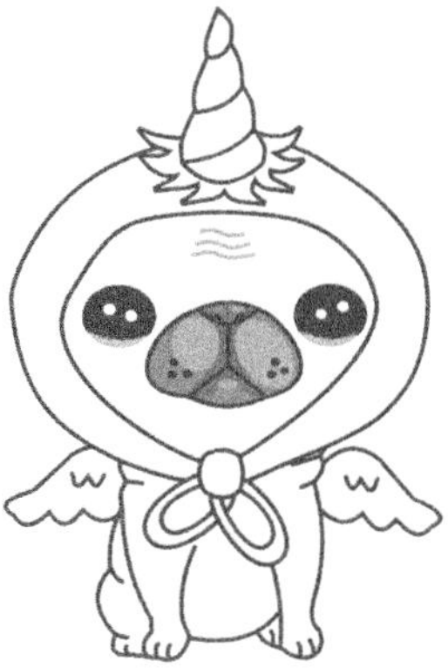
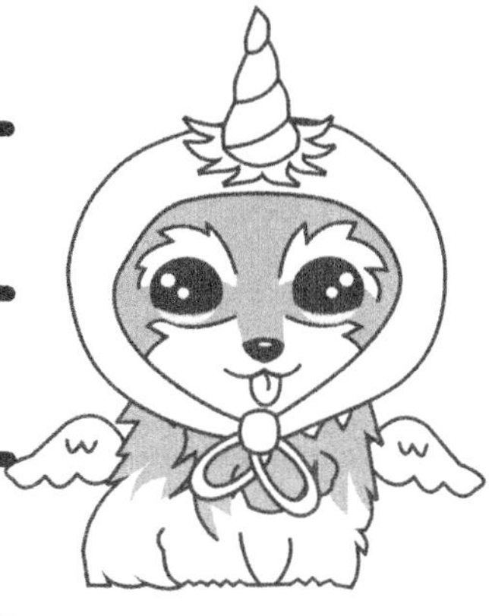

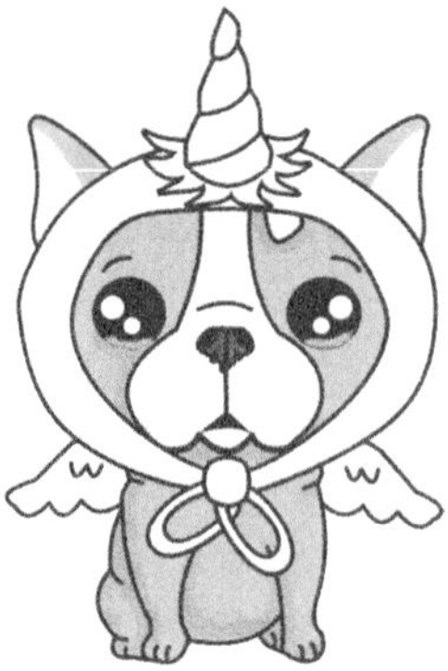

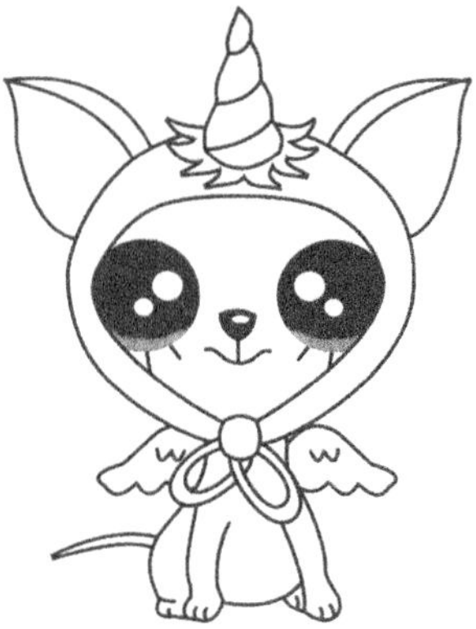

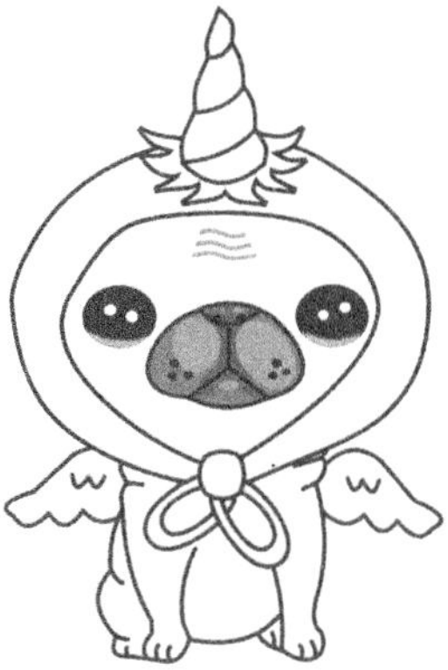

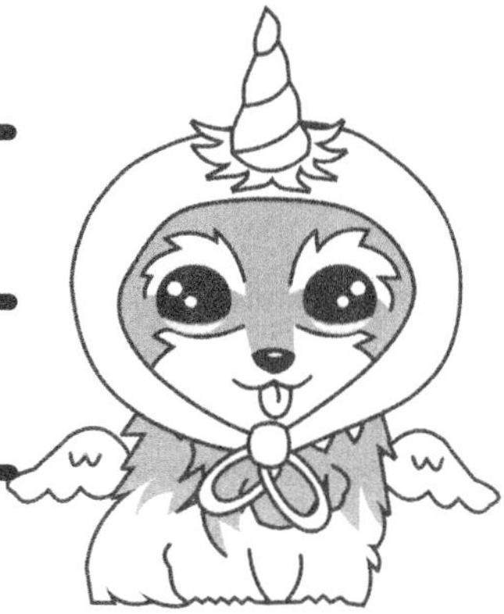

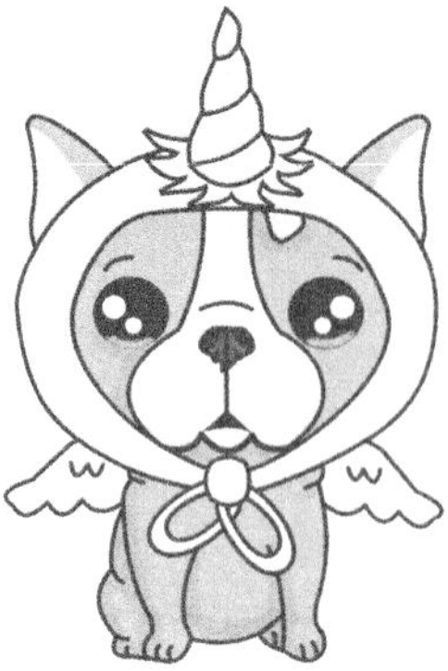

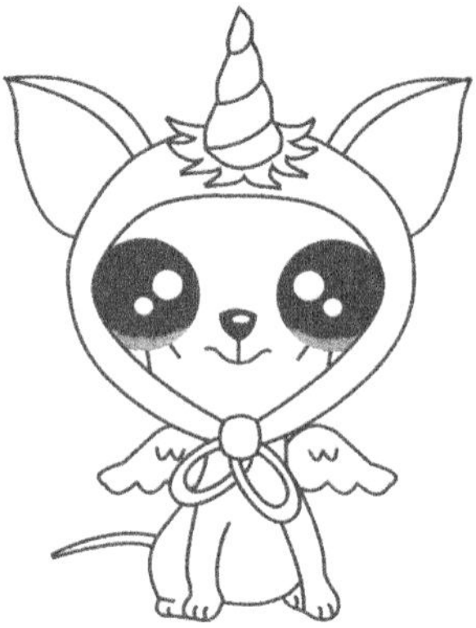

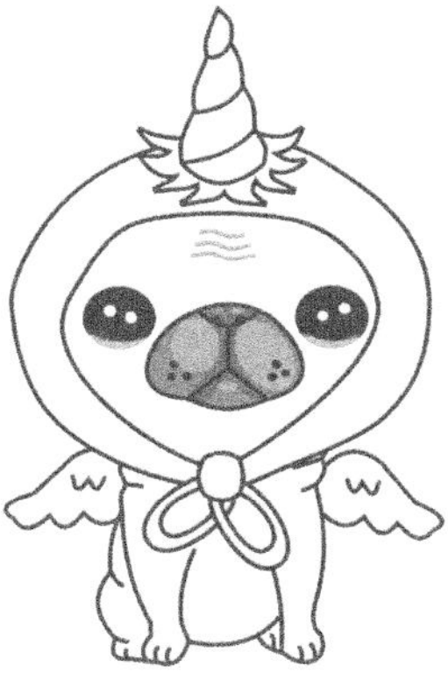

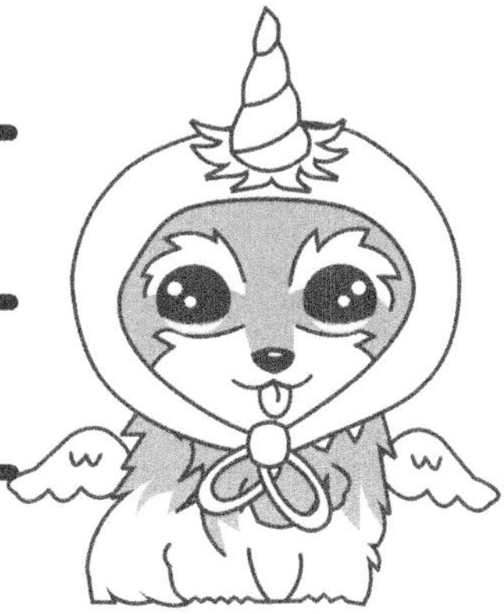

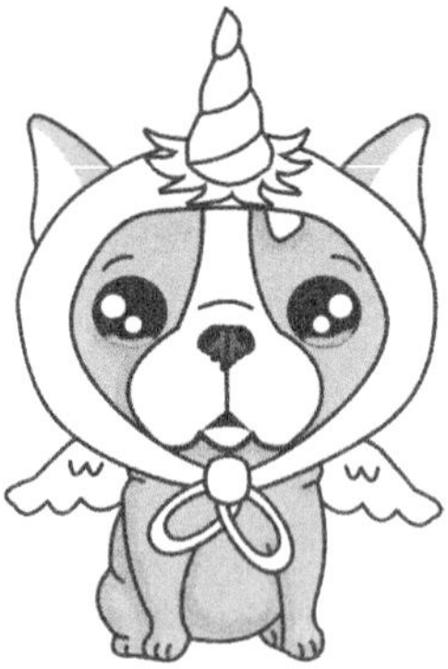

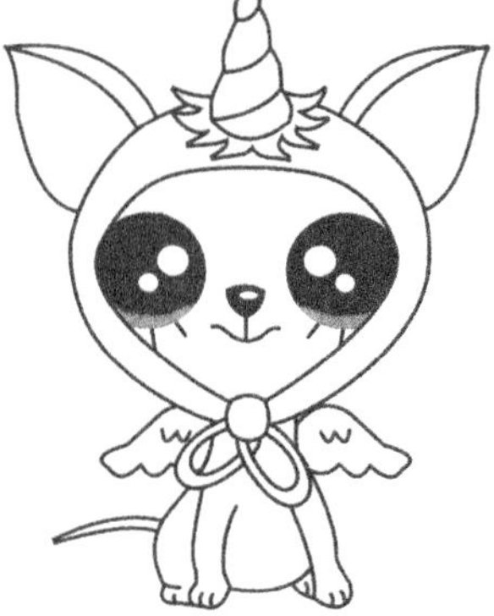

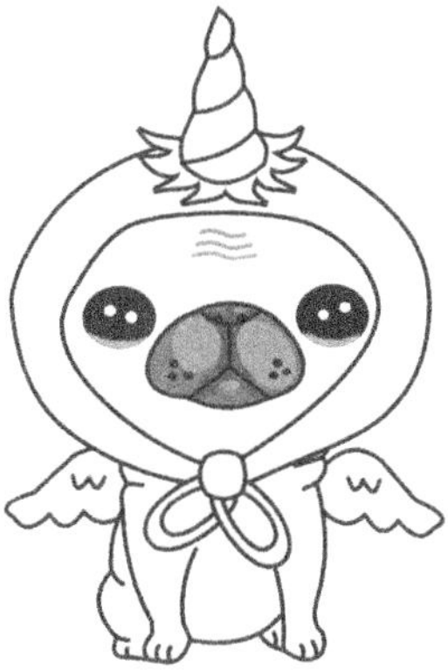

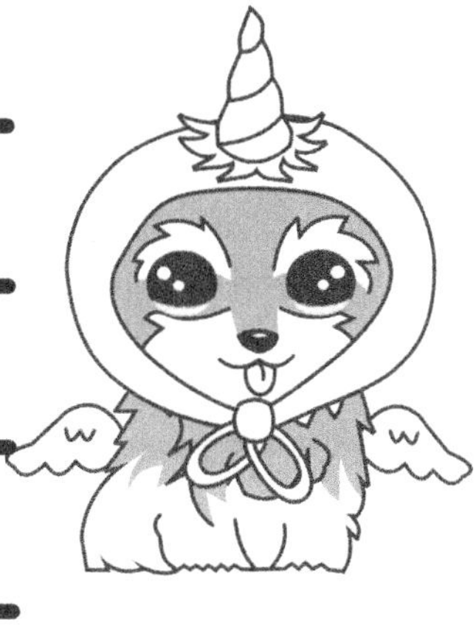

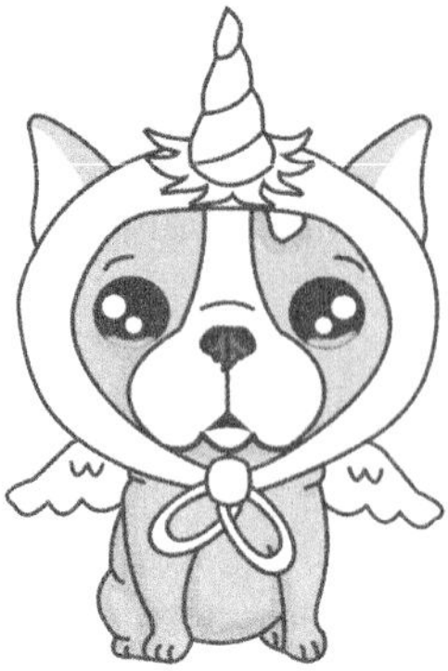

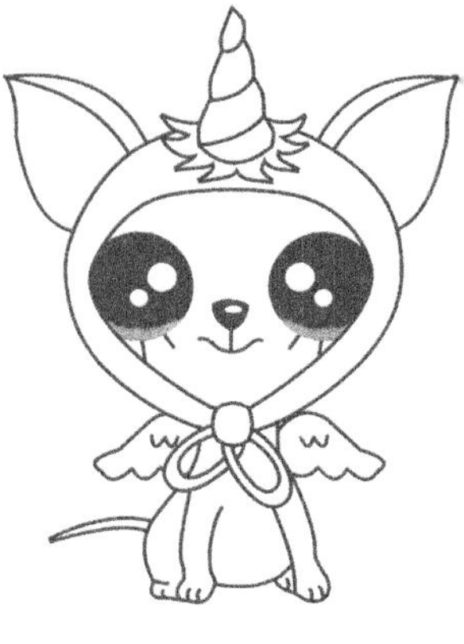

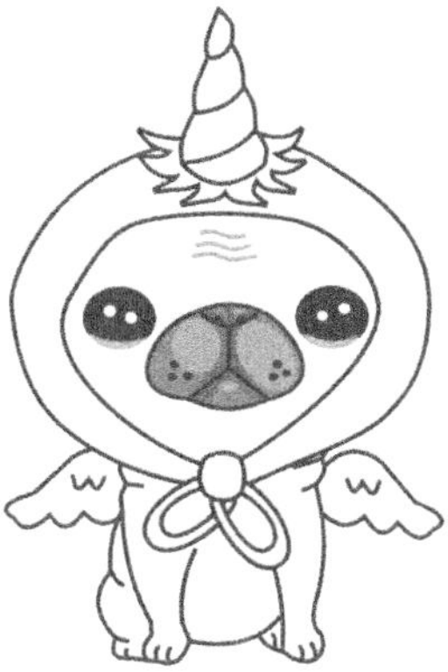

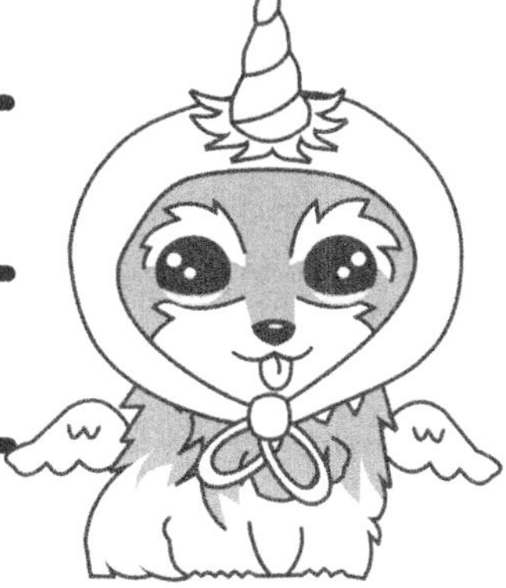

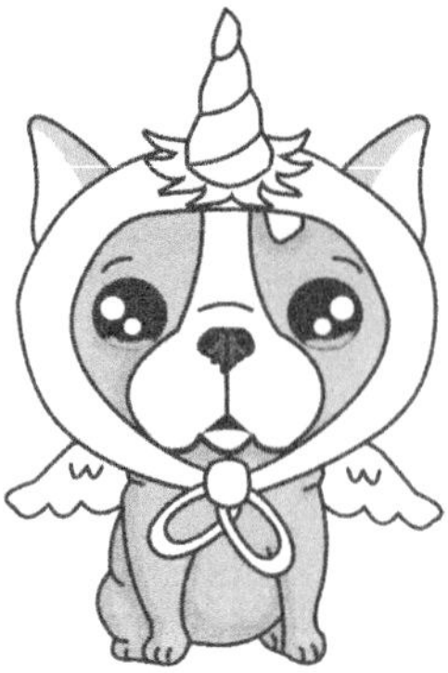

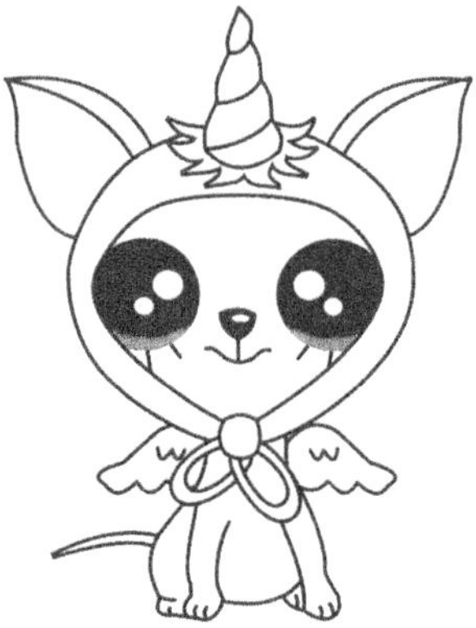

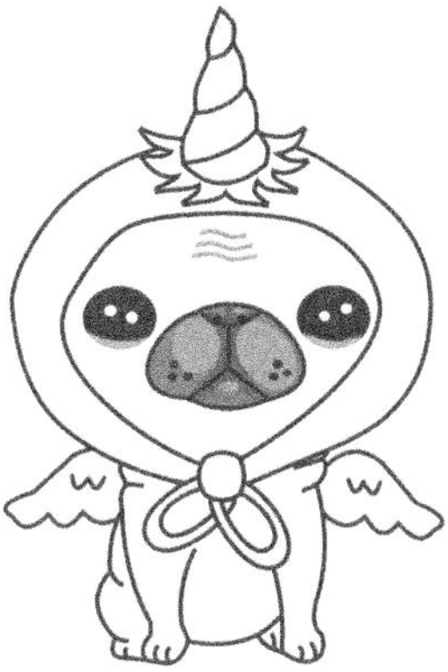

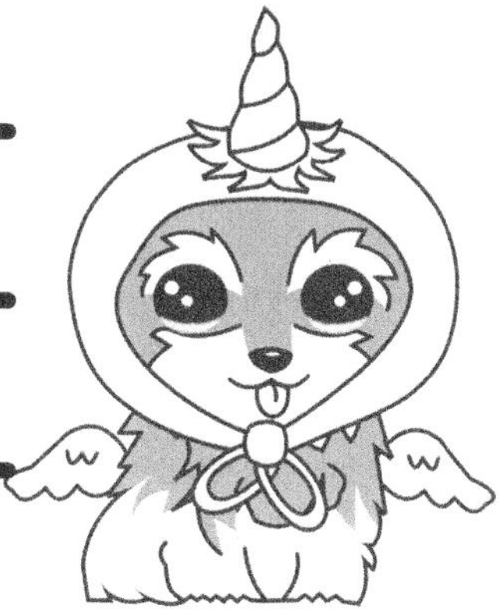

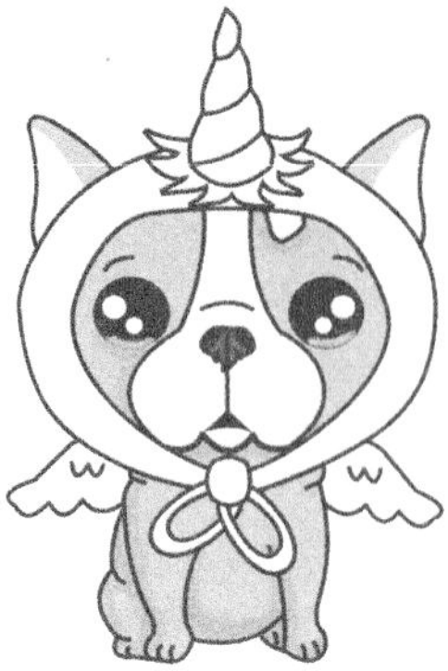

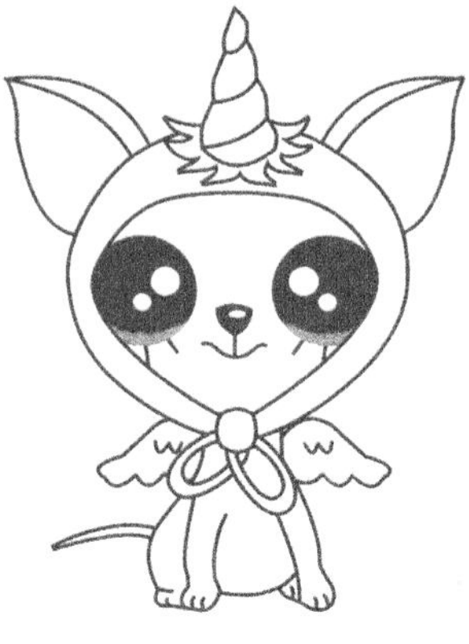

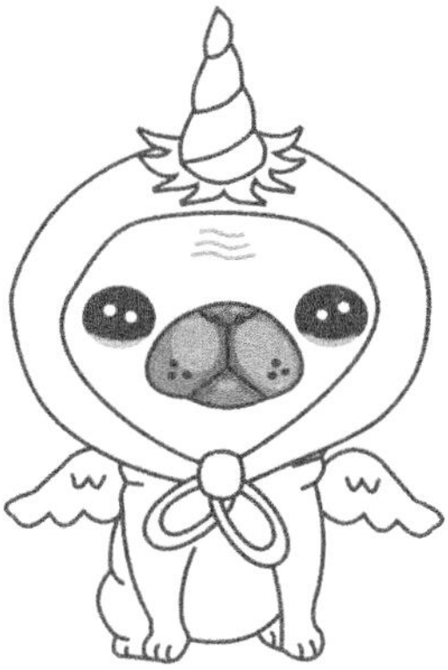

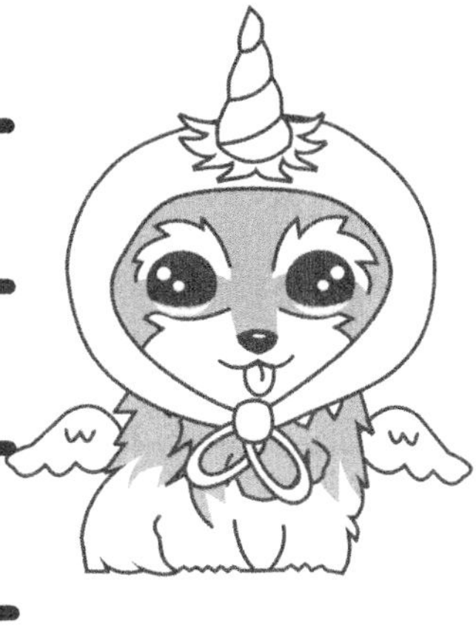

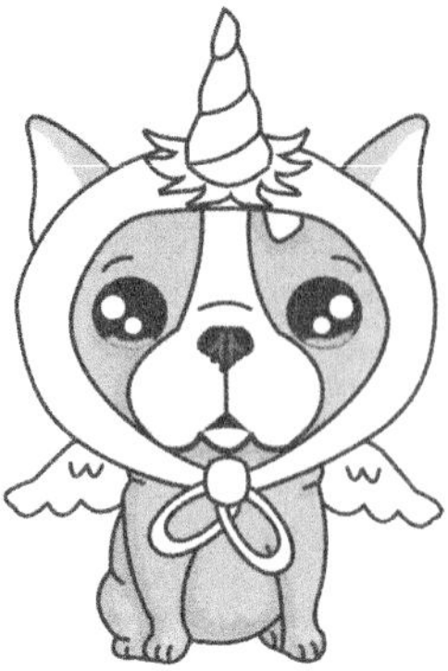

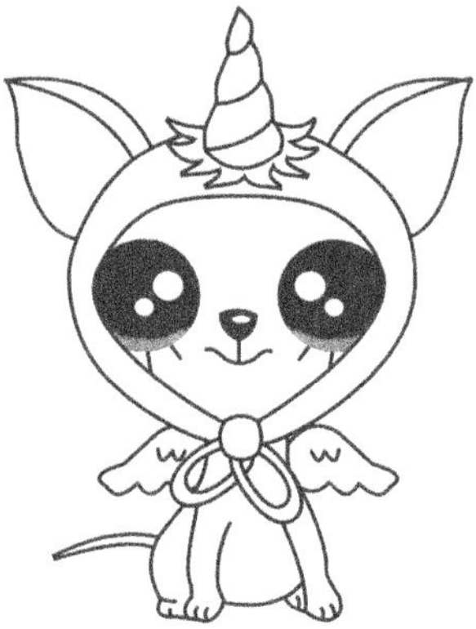

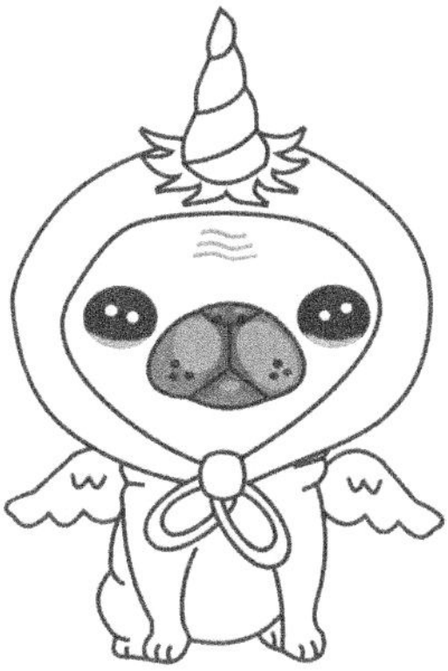

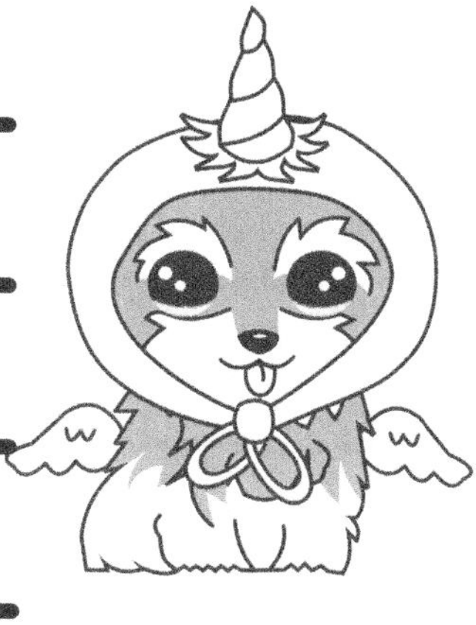

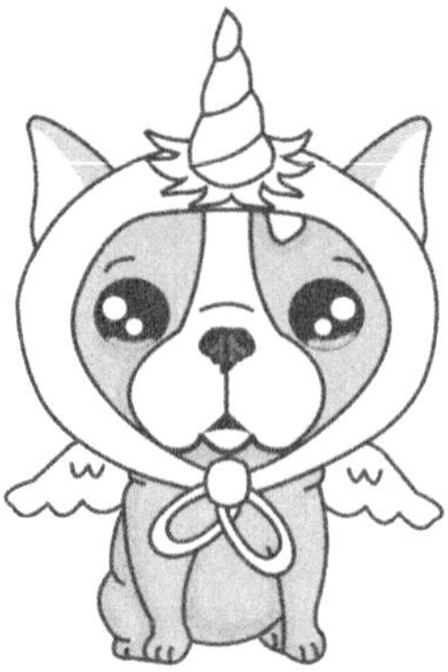

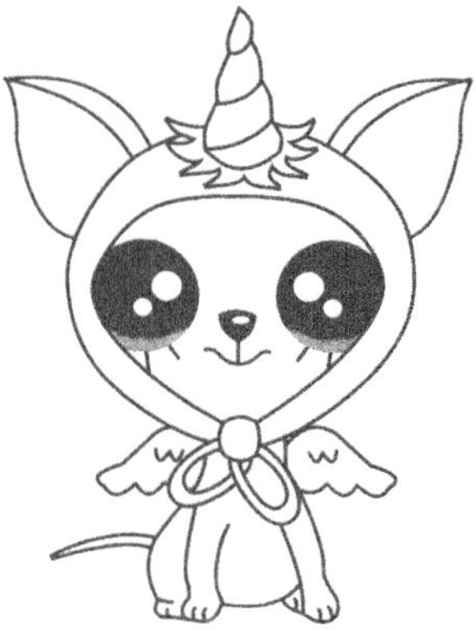

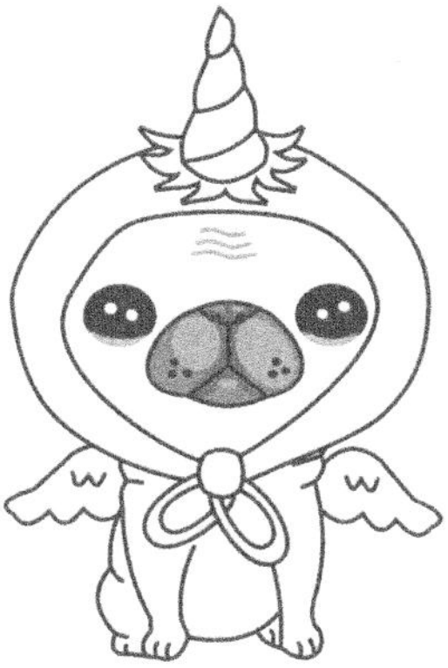
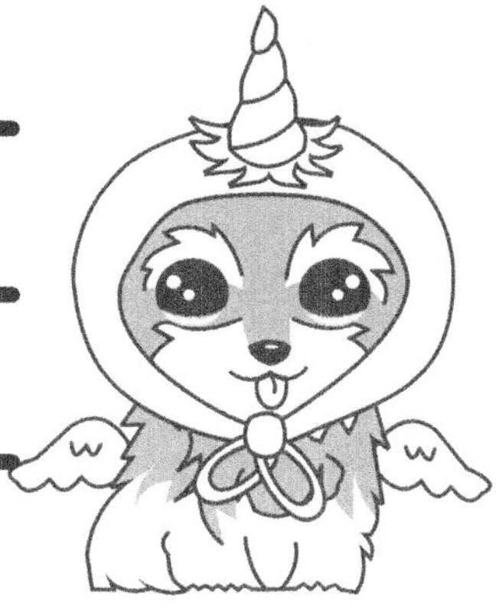

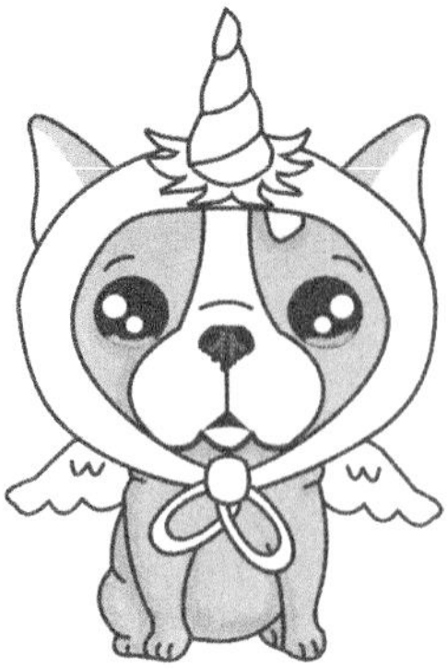

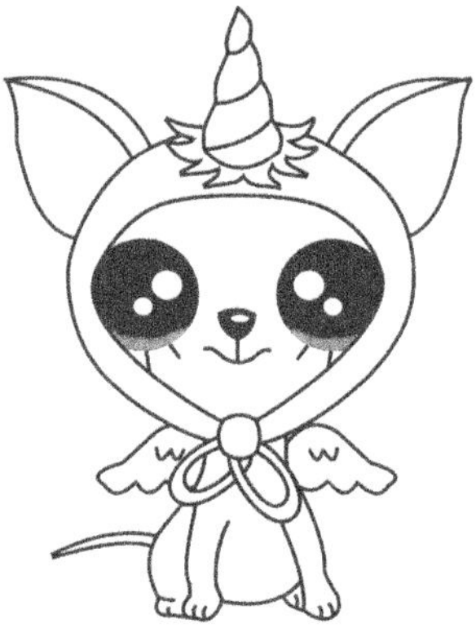

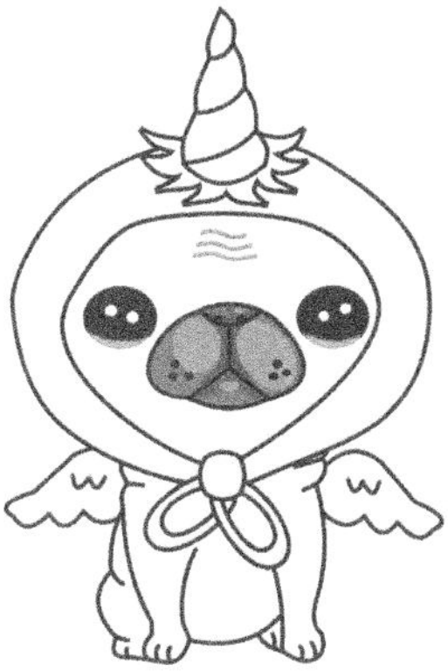

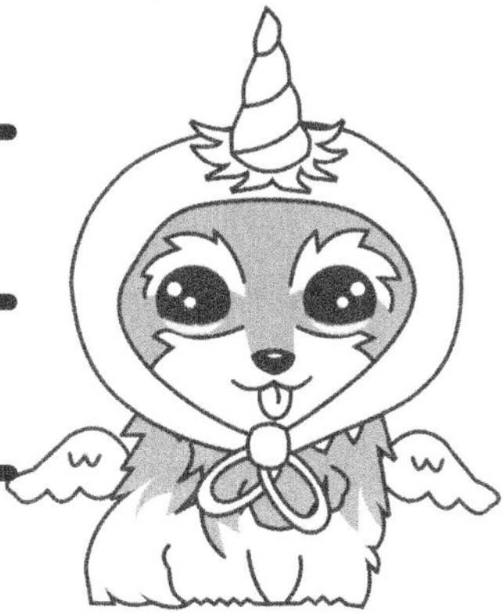

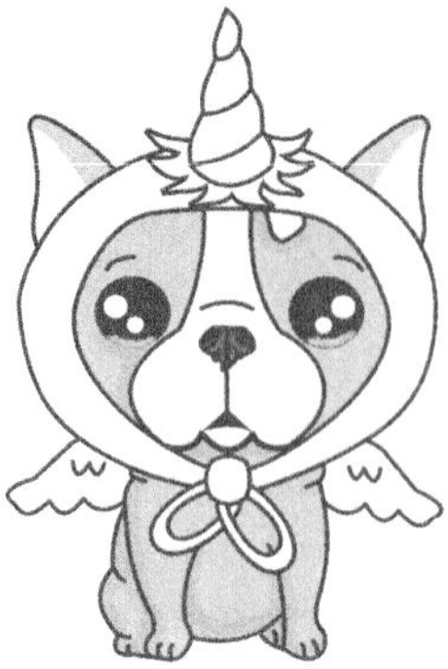

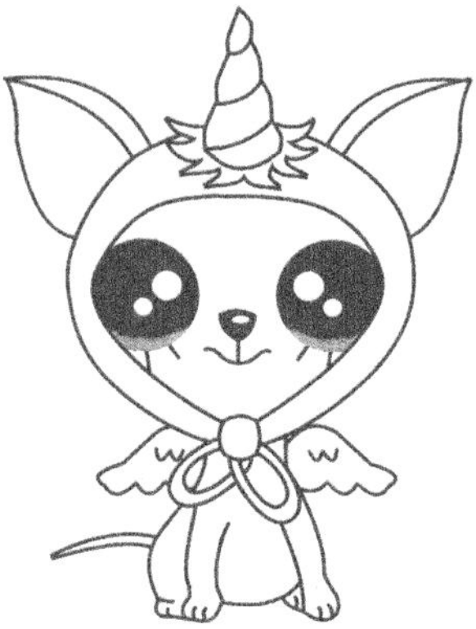

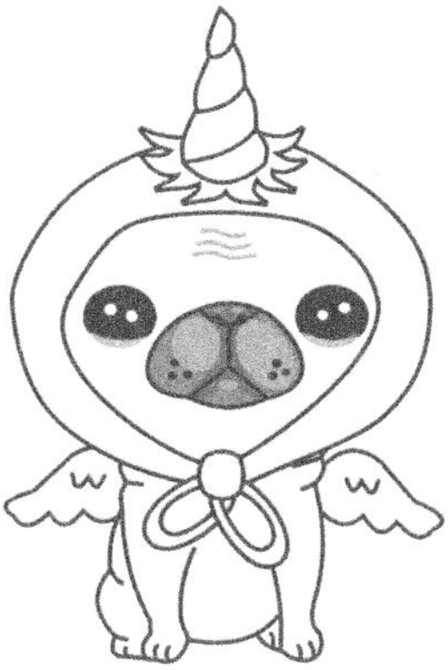

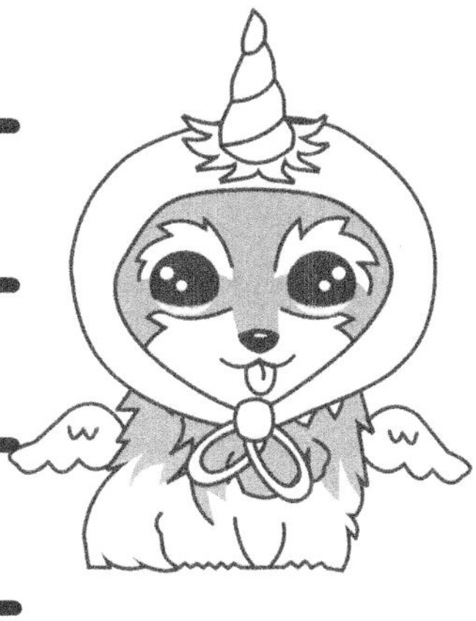

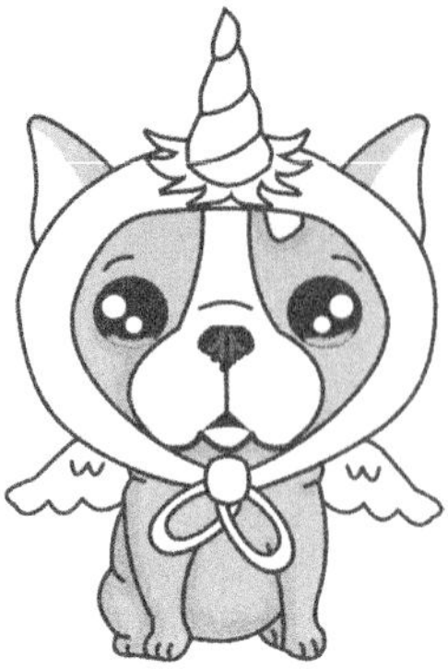

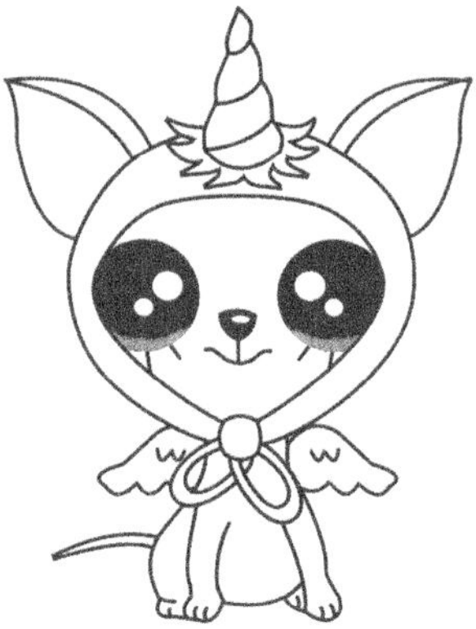

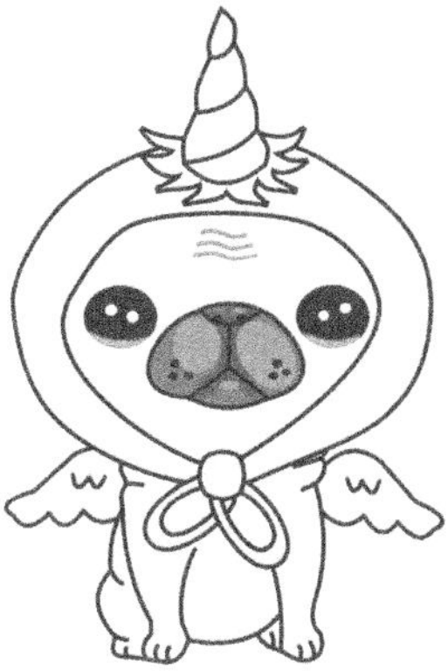

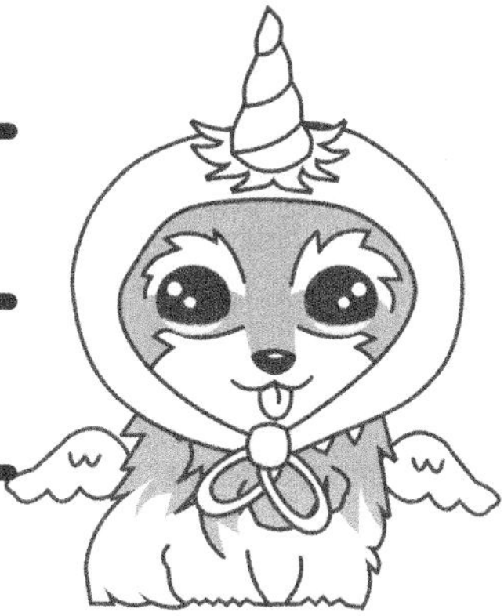

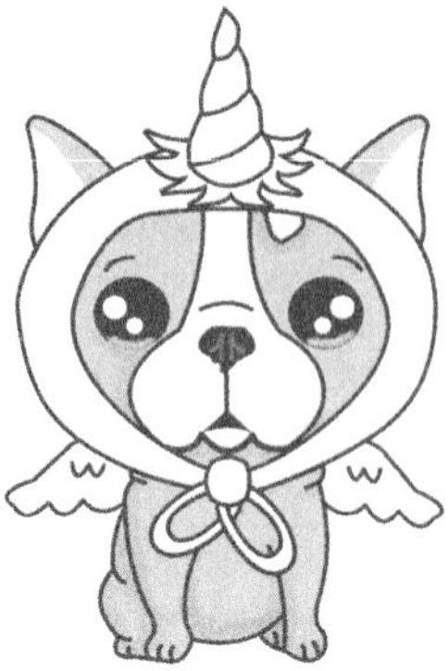

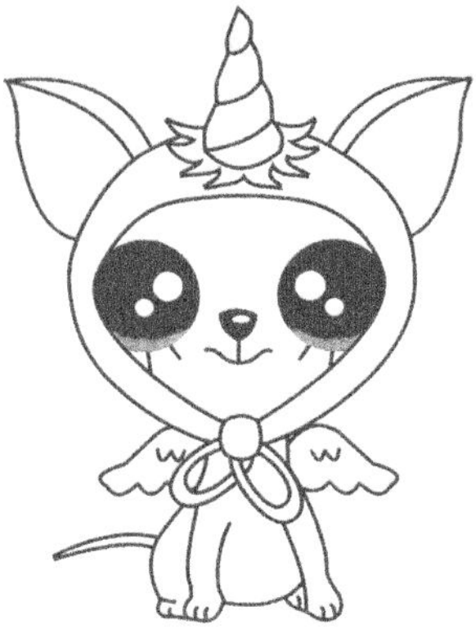

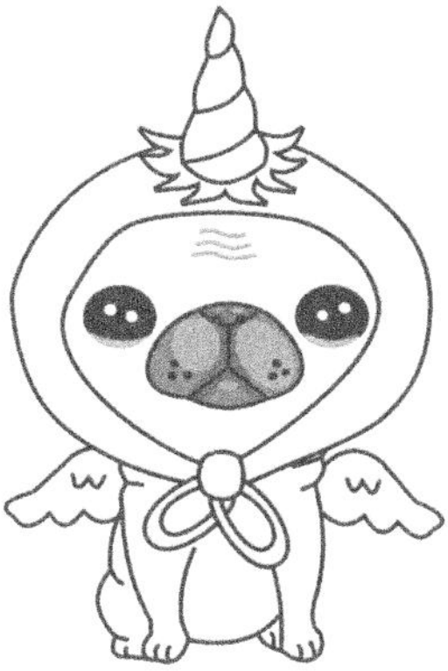

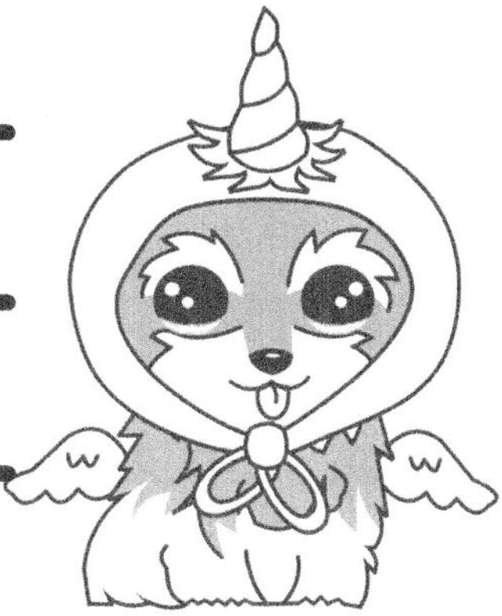

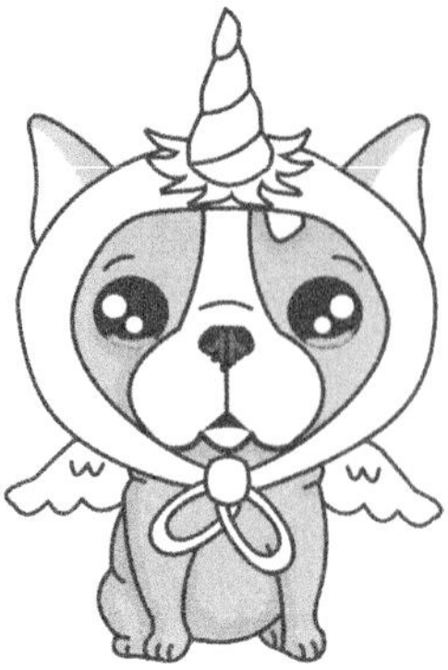
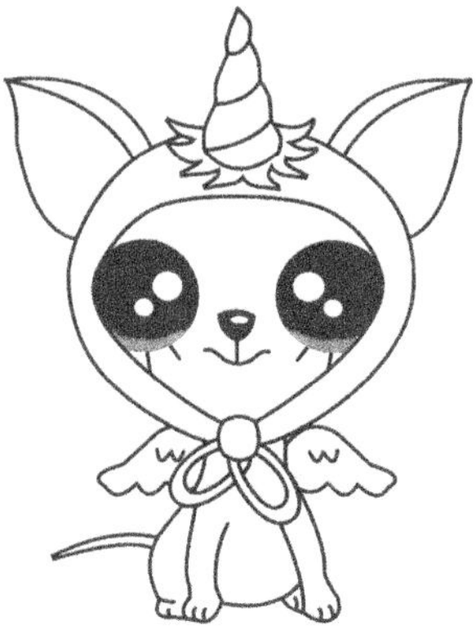

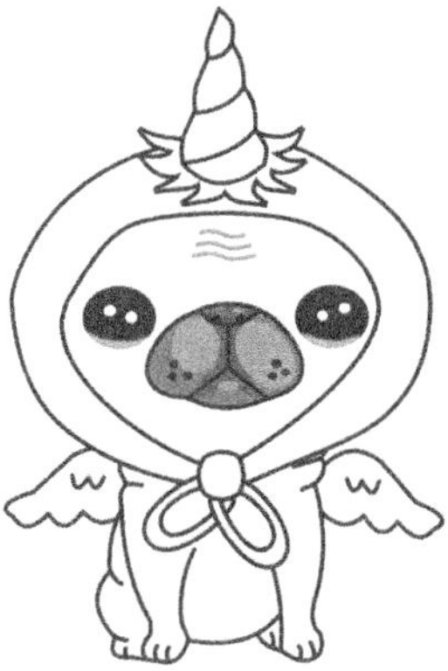

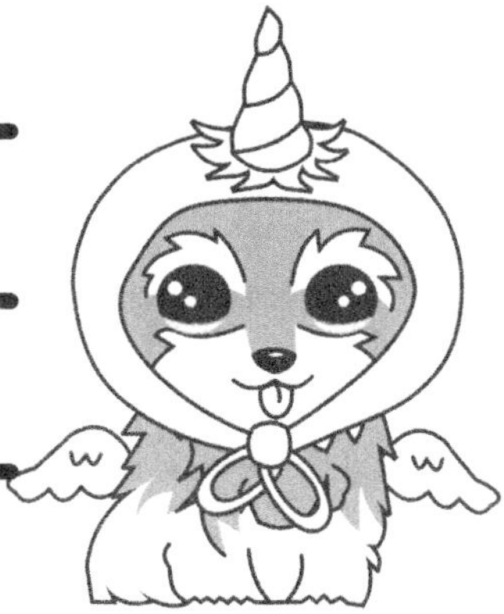

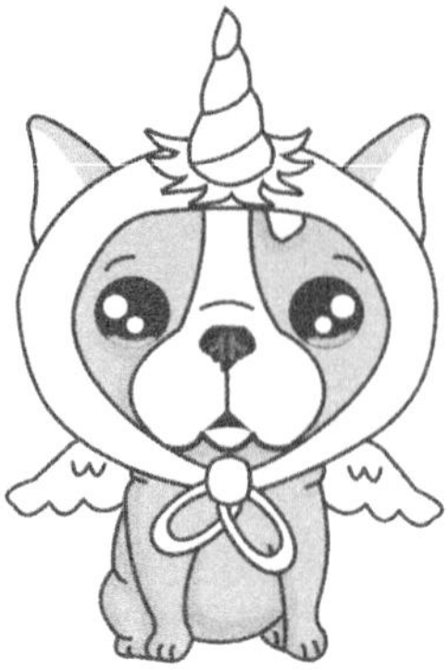

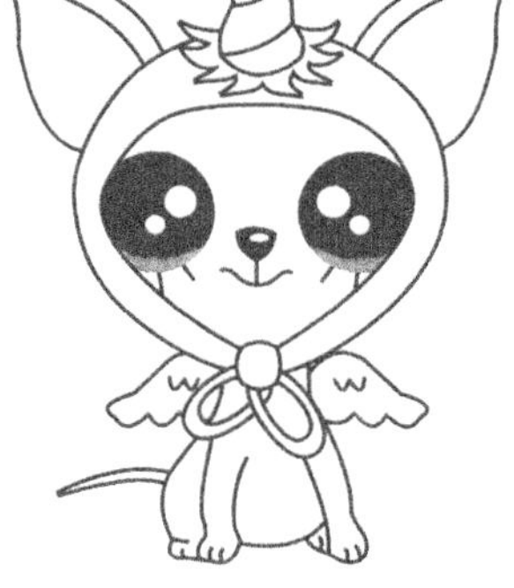

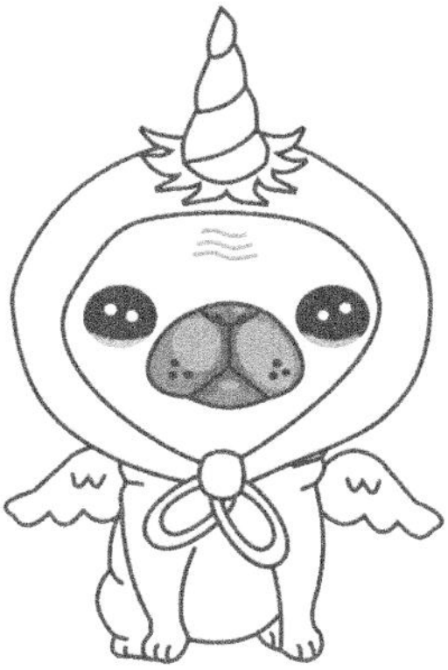

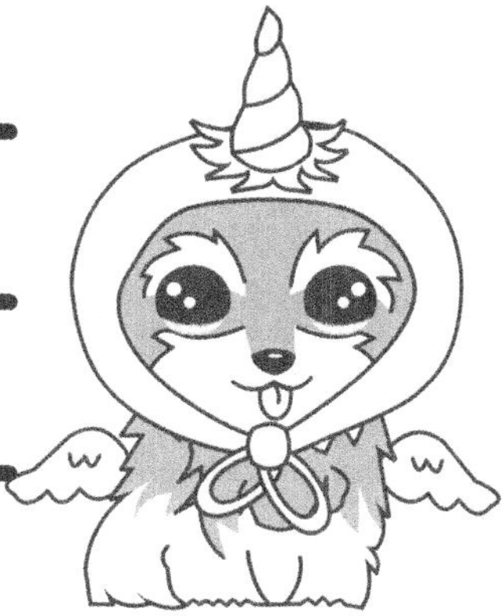

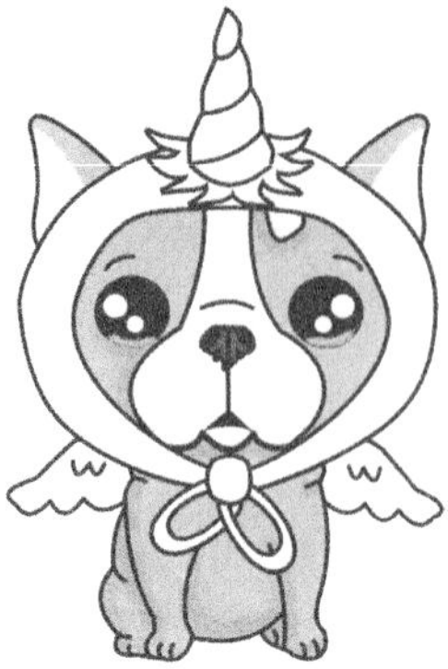

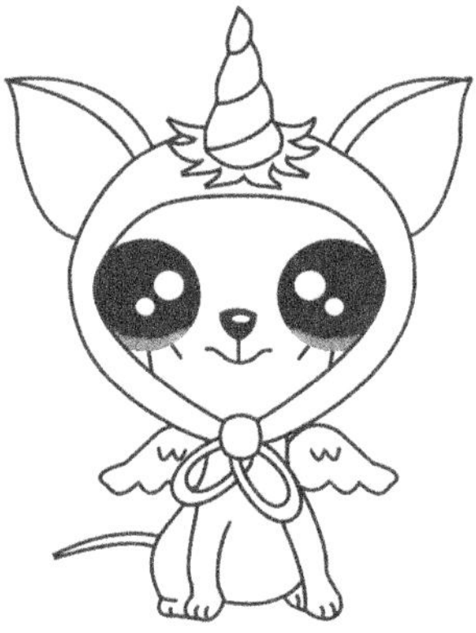

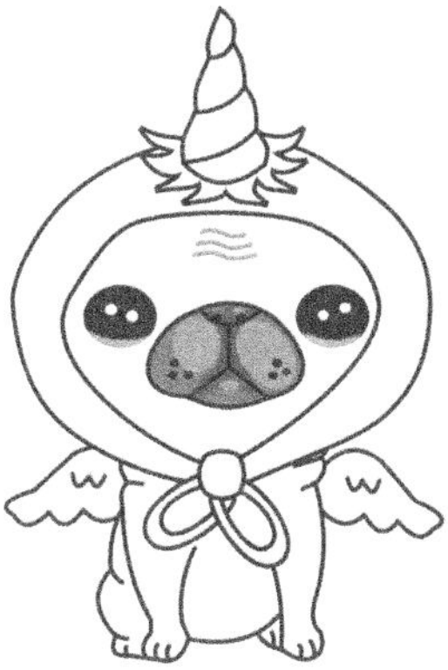

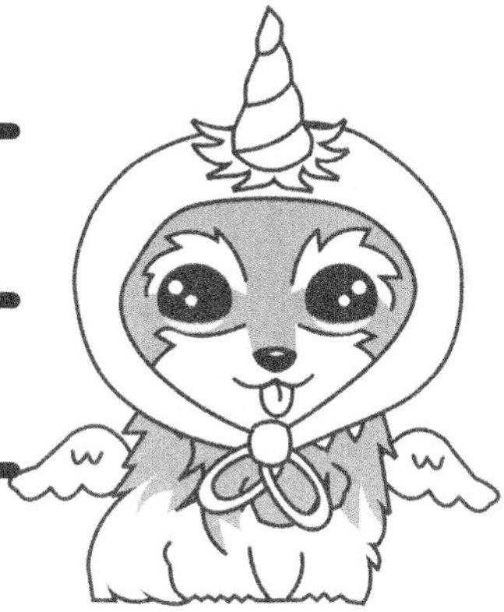

PLEASE DON'T DUPLICATE OR COPY THIS BOOK

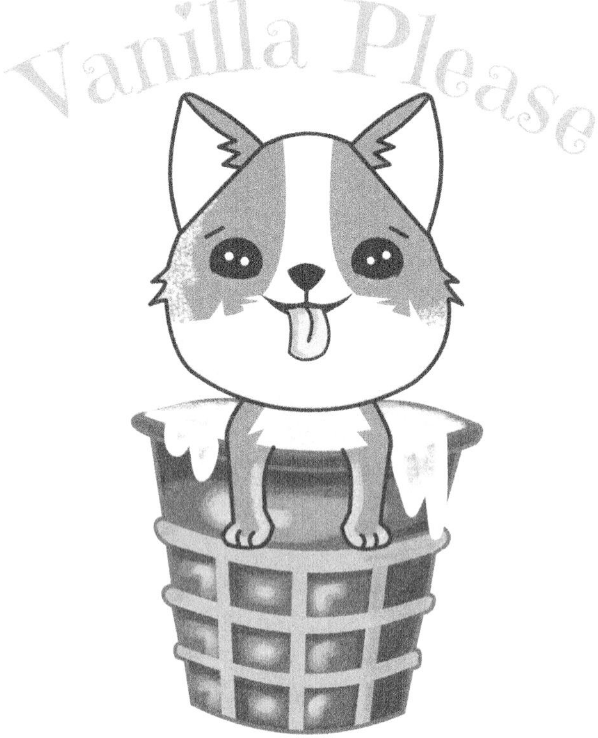

PLEASE CHECK OUT MY ADORABLE
PUPPY UNICORN
TEE SHIRTS BY MOOSING AROUND
ON AMAZON